Down the Town

By

Lorna Laidler

Published by LORWIL Publishing 2004
18 Crumstone Court
Killingworth
Newcastle upon Tyne
NE12 6SZ

ISBN 0-9546475-2-1

Printed in Great Britain by L&S Printers
Camperdown,
Tyne & Wear.
Tel. No. 0191 2161717

The Author aged 8

This book was written as a companion to 'Up The Valley', tales of childhood summers spent in Northumberland's upper Coquetdale.

It is the other side of my childhood, as the daughter of a policeman living around Newcastle, just after the war.

It is dedicated to my family of all generations.

Index

Poems

Drawings

Photographs

A FAIR SWAP?

"Accrington Stanley, one. Blackburn Rovers, one." Intoned the man on the wireless in the particular sing song voice he reserved for announcing a draw. You could always tell whether the other team had won, lost or drawn, by the way his voice rose or fell when announcing its name. Wireless broadcasts of football matches and the ensuing results were the invariable background against which Mam's' Saturday afternoon baking stint took place in the back kitchen of our terraced house on Tyneside. Not that she was interested in football mind you, but my father was a policeman, and worked shifts, so she was delegated to report on the prowess or otherwise of Newcastle United, and to mark the all important football coupon.

This piece of paper was regarded with awe verging on reverence. It held the promise, or at least the possibility, of riches beyond the dreams of avarice, so the minute the classified results began, the wireless was turned up, Mam wiped the flour from her hands, licked the end of a stub of indelible pencil, and gave the football coupon her undivided attention.

Her hunched figure crouched over the kitchen table marking the coupon this particular Saturday, when I wandered in beaming with pride at my business acumen. I was under four years old but even then, knew better than to interrupt the pools results, so, hitching from one leg to the other in the back doorway, I waited impatiently for the moment when I could show Mam the brilliant swap I'd made.

For a tiny little ring with a small squiggle of sparkly bits I had got this magnificent toy car! It was blue and shiny with real rubber tyres. I twiddled the wheels with my finger and glowed with satisfaction. The man on the wireless droned to a conclusion and Mam stood up, put both hands in the small of her back and grimaced as she stretched to ease her discomfort.

The cause of her discomfort was a bump on her tummy. I had noticed Mam's tummy getting bigger lately. It made sitting on her knee most uncomfortable, gave Mam a bad back, and was altogether most inconvenient. She had murmured little confidences about a baby brother or sister, but I dismissed these as adult ramblings.

Mam pushed the football coupon away and turned to see me hopping in the doorway, my prize held out for inspection.

"Lucka this Mam, lucka this bonny car I got off Danny."
Instead of the expected smile of congratulation, an expression of anxiety settled on Mam's face.

"What did Danny give you his car for? You'll have to give him it back, or his mammy will be cross.

In these post war years toys were precious and parents were apt to hammer angrily on the doors of houses thought to harbour the purloined playthings of their children.

"It's all right mammy. I did a swap." I announced with confidence. Suspicion immediately replaced anxiety on Mam's face as she asked, " What did you swap it for? Not your bike!"

A silly question, as nothing would have induced me to part with my rusty third hand tricycle.

Me on my treasured tricycle in the back yard at Newburn

"No, I just swapped that ring off the back kitchen window sill."
I was astonished at the outcome of this harmless piece of information. Mam's left hand flew up as she glanced at the naked ring finger. She darted to the windowsill and grabbed gratefully at the plain band of gold still lying there. (It had seemed too ordinary to me to be worth swapping for anything and so had been reprieved.) Mam was in the habit of removing her wedding and engagement rings at the beginning of each baking session to prevent them getting clogged with flour. Having no idea of the importance of these bits of metal, I had picked up the prettier of the two and the transaction with the toy car had followed.
"Me engagement ring!" croaked Mam, a look of anguish on her face. "Where does Danny live? Quick, I'll have to get it back before your dad comes home."
"What's an engagement ring? " I asked
"It's something very special that you keep for always." Mam replied. "Quick now, where does Danny live? We'll have to give him his car and get me ring back."

My face crumpled and I pulled the beautiful blue car to my chest, giving it one last hug before the inevitable parting. Mam's face softened and she knelt down beside me.

"I'm sorry pet. It's a lovely car, but I have to get my engagement ring back, it is very special to me, like————like." She groped for an example of something equally precious to me, "like Sambo is special to you," she finished. That clinched it. Sambo was my black doll, (named before political correctness reared its head.) I loved, cherished and was as proud of him as any mother of a gifted child. If this ring was as important as Sambo all the stops would have to be pulled out to retrieve it.

"Now, where does Danny live?" asked Mam gently.

"In the next street," I replied through trembling lips, Mam's face blurred as the tears formed in my eyes.

"Clever girl, .Now, which way? The next street up the hill, or the next street that way or that way?" Asked Mam, pointing in the three possible directions.

"I don't know," I wailed "I was playing with him at the top of our street, so he must come from the next street."

My childish logic was based on the fact that, in our area of streets running down to the banks of the Tyne, young children played with denizens of their own street, or sometimes the street adjoining, but very rarely with anyone farther afield. Two streets away were foreign parts for three and four year olds.

Helpless desperation best describes Mam's expression as she rose to her feet.

"Stay here till I come back." She called, rushing out of the back door, across the concrete yard, blue car clutched in her hand. At the yard gate she stopped dead in her tracks and dashed back.

"The scones!" She muttered, hauling open the door to the gas oven. Hot scones were tumbled out onto the kitchen table, The old grey gas oven was turned off with a pop and a splutter and Mam darted out of the house again. It took forty five minutes of running up and down the steeply sloping streets before she tracked down Danny, a big boy of six, who had an inkling of the value of engagement rings, and was non too keen to part with it. A swift skelp around the ear from his Mam gave him the necessary incentive to relinquish it, whereupon he was reunited with his blue car.

Mam returned, tired but triumphant and was able to present a picture of untroubled serenity to my father when he came home at the end of his shift.

Goodness knows why I was so desperate to acquire that car. I was a fortunate child in that I actually owned two dolls, a rarity just after the war. One was a very plain creature with a bald head, called Joan. Later dolls had stuck on heads of brown hair, which I quickly brushed into oblivion, but my favourite was Sambo.

He was a small black doll, dressed in a bright red knitted suit, complete with beret, which he wore at a jaunty angle. I adored him and fussed endlessly, tucking him into bed and hauling him out again.

That summer was warm, so reasoning that Sambo obviously came from Africa, which I knew was hot, (an adult cousin sent frequent bulletins from The Sudan, where she was teaching.) I decided that he might like to do a spot of sunbathing in the back yard.

Sambo was carefully arranged on an old tea towel in the sunniest corner, his red clothes making a bright splash of colour in the monochrome surroundings. Side tracked to another game in the back lane, poor Sambo was forgotten, until hours later, running past him, my steps faltered. Something was wrong. The beret's normally jaunty angle was looking decidedly sad. Closer inspection revealed that poor old Sambo had melted! Nothing was left but a gooey mess welded into his beautiful red suit! He looked just like a half chewed treacle toffee.

I missed Sambo a lot, but at least I didn't resort to the remedy my Coquet valley cousin, Bob employed. Lord alone knows what inspired him to do it, but he found a paint brush and a tin of "Darkolene" and proceeded early one morning to paint his baby sister brown! Baby Betty's cries of outrage thankfully brought aunty Peg running before the job was completed.

Darkolene was used in those days to stain any floorboards left uncovered by the central square of lino or carpet, (fitted carpets were unheard of then) so it took Aunty Peg some time to undo Bob's handiwork. She would be amazed to see the current fashion for bare floorboards, stained or otherwise.

As a result of all the running about though, Mam's bump caused her something more productive than backache. Within the next twenty-four hours I was packed off to stay with another policeman and his wife who lived four streets away. (Foreign parts indeed.) Mam went off to her mother's in South Shields, and there my little sister, Linda was born somewhat earlier than had been anticipated

THE PREFAB

For most of my child hood I was one of a pair, but I do have a few vague memories of the time when I was the one and only

When I was a baby, my father, like many dads those days was in the army, so Mam and I spent our time shuttling between the contrasting homes of my two nanas. The one on Mam's side, nana Nicholson, lived in South Shields in a neat little house full of female relatives. (Mam had a plethora of wonderful sisters)

Robbie, Nana, Eva, Agnes (in uniform), Nora and cousin Ann in front

The one on dad's side, nana Nairn, lived on a hill farm in the depths of Northumberland with my granda and dad's two brothers.

It is a wonder I didn't develop a schizophrenic personality, as, in the differing lifestyles of town and country, I have always had a foot in both camps.

Down The Town

It was while Mam and I were staying with the country branch of the family that news came through to South Shields that we had been allocated a prefab of our own. Mam had to accept it within a few days, or it would go to the next person on the list .So my poor aunt Nora, never in the most robust of health, made the marathon journey from South Shields, through Newcastle and into the wilds of Northumberland to inform her sister of her good fortune and enable her to return to Shields in time to claim the prized prefab.

I know that it later became common to regard prefabs with scorn, but my earliest memories are of a cosy little home where Mam and I were content and comfortable. I didn't know then that such things as dads existed. My South Shields nana was a widow, so hers was an entirely female household.

My granda in the country was, well, granda. I never thought of him as being anyone's dad, I loved him and he loved me and that was that.

Mam and I were sufficient unto ourselves. From the prefab we paid regular visits to nana Nicholson nearby, where I enjoyed being surrounded by hoards of female relatives.

Mam's family on a trip to Marsden Beach

The kitchen of this nana's home was always full to overflowing with children of all ages.

The babble of conversation was constant and Nana presided over her many children and grandchildren, dispensing love common sense and wisdom from her chair by the hearth.

I enjoyed these visits so much, that one day I decided to make the trip on my own. Sitting my teddy bear in the pushchair, I set off from our prefab. It had seemed a short journey when I went with Mam, so I stepped out confidently, hands stretched high to reach the handle of the pushchair, face peering over its back, like Chad looking over a wall.

Perhaps it was because I couldn't see where I was going very well that I got completely lost. As my predicament dawned on me, anxiety began to set in. I wasn't really frightened yet though, my experience of adults thus far had been such that they represented security.

The streets down which I pushed my teddy bear were full of adults, so the answer to the problem seemed simple — ask one of them for help. I stopped beside a woman donkey stoning her front step,

"Please, I'm lost."

"Oh aye?" This without breaking the rhythm of her scrubbing.

"Can you show me how to get home? I live in Mitchell Gardens." (I'd given up the idea of visiting Nana by this time.) She lifted her head on which a scarf battened down rows of tight metal curlers.

" De yee think a've got nowt better to dee wi me time than run aboot the streets wi daft bairns? Hadaway hyem! A'm busy!"

"I was absolutely bewildered by her attitude, and frightened.

My assumption that the world was full of kind caring people had been rudely shattered. Thus, at the age of three, I came to the awful realisation that it was, in fact, fraught with danger, and contained some people who were not very nice.

The nasty woman

"With thudding heart and fluttering stomach, I reflected on my foolish adventure and pointed my pushchair down yet another unfamiliar street, trying, without success, to stem the tears of panic. After a few very long minutes, an elderly gentleman crouched down beside me. His tweed cap and jacket reminded me of my country granda and I immediately put my trust in him.

"What's the matter hinny? Yer a little titch of a lass to be oot on yer awn. Are yee lost?"

I nodded dumbly, unable yet to speak through my distress.

"Right! Now yer little bits o' legs 'll be worn oot wi walkin'. Sit doon in yer push chair and see if yee can tell me where yee live." He pushed my teddy into my arms and lifted me carefully into the pushchair.

"What's yer name bonny lass?"
"Norny," I replied, this being the way I pronounced my name.
"And do yee knaa where yee live?"
"Mitchell Gardens." I replied.

Fortunately, I was more adept at pronouncing my address than my name, so within a short time my saviour had wheeled me back to the prefab, where my distraught mother had roused the neighbours and was about to inform the police. The kind man did much to restore my faith in humanity, but the encounter with the donkey stone woman severely dented my child's trust in mankind.

Those early years in the prefab must have been quite a trial for my mother. She had only me and a grey kitten called Whisky to look after, but both Whisky and I contrived to keep her on her toes. The very first thing the kitten did was sneak into the airing cupboard and from there, somehow insinuate himself into the fabric of the building! Major excavations were carried out before he was rescued.

Strict rationing was in force then. Eggs were as precious as opals, so one of my early efforts at cordon bleu was not greeted with the appreciation I had anticipated. The newly acquired egg ration lay in the middle of the table, next to them, a bottle of ink, which Mam had been using to write to dad, still away in the Coldstream Guards. My embryonic creative instinct stirred, and I rummaged about in the cupboard until I found a mixing bowl.

Heaving it up onto the table, I climbed onto a chair. Carefully, I broke all the eggs into the bowl and didn't let one piece of egg shell mar the purity of that wonderful glutinous mixture! I stirred it with a fork, fascinated by the way each yellow yolk broke and bled into the whites. It was really very pretty, but could be improved on I thought.

Casting around for something to brighten the mixture, my eye fell on the bottle of ink. Perfect! The lid was mutinous, but I wrestled with it and won. The ink was a resounding success, it swirled through the egg in streams of blue ranging in tone from midnight, through sky to turquoise and green. Magnificent! Pride in my creation was short lived. Mam came into the room and was understandably dismayed to see her entire egg ration adulterated by ink. She told everyone later that I'd been trying to make an omelette. I hugged my secret to me. It wasn't an omelette. It was a work of art!

The existence of my father filtered through to my consciousness only very slowly. Mam talked about him a lot and he managed to get home occasionally, but I have no memory of him until a visit he made to the prefab. He was ill with jaundice, so spent most of the time in bed. To me, he was a stranger, glimpsed from the bedroom doorway. I suppose he must have talked to me, but I have no recollection of any real interaction, until the day Mam popped out to the local shop to replenish out food supplies while my father was sleeping.

Playing quietly with my toys in the living room, I heard my father's voice calling faintly. I trotted to the bedroom door. He was lying there looking very weak and faintly yellow, waving his empty glass towards me.

"Can you get me a drink pet, I'm thirsty."

I took the glass, extremely proud to be asked to help, and returned gravely bearing it, half full. He propped himself up on one elbow and gratefully drank the lot before sinking back onto the pillow.

"Thanks," he gasped, eyes closed, beads of perspiration glistening on his forehead and top lip. Suddenly, his eyes flew open and he turned to look at me,

"Can you reach the tap?" He asked.

"No, I'm too little."

"Well where did you get the water from?"

"Down the toilet." I replied, proud of my initiative

"Bloody hell." He murmured with resignation, and went to sleep.

The Drink

THE DRINK

My soldier dad, just home from war
Had taken to his bed.
His skin gave off a yellow glow,
"Jaundice!" The doctor said.

Mam tended him with loving care
Until she had to pop
For badly needed food supplies
Just to the local shop.

"Your father's fast asleep" she said,
"I know you're only three,
But be a big girl for your Mam
And watch your dad for me."

I sat myself upon the floor
Beside my father's bed
Mam had not been gone for long
When father lifts his head.

"Water, water, please." He cried
"Go get your dad a drink"
So off I went and, cup in hand,
I toddled to the sink

The trouble was, I couldn't reach
To turn the water on
I heard my father's feeble voice,
"Come on lass, where've you gone?"

Down The Town

Desperation led my feet
Right through the bathroom door,
I found some water I could reach
Much nearer to the floor.

Bearing the brimming cup before,
I offered it with pride.
He drank, sank back onto the bed,
Closed up his eyes and sighed.

And then, his eyes snapped open,
"Where did you get that drink?
I should have thought before I asked
You cannot reach the sink."

"I didn't get your water from the sink,"
Was what I said.
"Well where?" The weak rejoinder
From the figure on the bed.

"I got it from the netty
If you want to know the truth."
Then I watched in some amazement
As my father hit the roof.

Down The Town

Dad in his army uniform with me as a baby

NEWBURN

When my father was demobbed and joined the Northumberland County Constabulary, our first home together as a family was a terraced house in Newburn in one of several rows sloping down to the north bank of the Tyne. The streets were so steep that to stand at the top and look down was to invite an attack of vertigo! The houses too had a decided lean to starboard. When my baby sister was born, her pram was prone to free wheel from the front door right across the living room to the chimney wall, unless kept a firm grip on, or the brakes applied.

The living room had a fireplace, a black leaded effort, with an oven at one side. On winter mornings my vests were hung on the oven door to warm, bliss! The kitchen was not graced with that name, we called it the scullery. There were two bedrooms upstairs, washing was done at the kitchen sink, bathing, in a tin bath in front of the fire, and the lavatory, although of the flushing variety, was at the end of the back yard, next to the coalhouse.

The front door let straight out onto the street, covered in loose stones, which we children used as currency, or goods in our play shops. Looking back, it amazes me that the only thing we never did with those stones was throw them. There were one or two real scallywags in Davison Street too, yet I don't remember the eminently throwable stones being used as missiles at all. Remarkable really, but in those days children had "rails to run on" and knew what the result of transgressions would be!

This stony street was fringed by anonymous terraced houses, the only identifying feature of each one being the colour of its front door, and, in the absence of gardens, the care, or otherwise, lavished on the front door step. Cardinal red was popular and most mornings saw turbaned housewives crouched down reddening their steps (and their knees.) Some favoured the donkey stone. This bestowed a creamy colour and the fashion was for the step to be edged with a line of cream applied with precision that would have been the envy of any draftsman.

The fashion in front doors ran to a paint effect that attempted to imitate wood grain. In actual fact they looked as though someone had poured a tin of treacle down them, but the possessors of these syrupy front doors were immensely proud of them.

These streets were to be the nucleus of my world for the next three years. Our street began half way down the slope with a traditional corner shop, the block on the first part of the slope being occupied by the Methodist Chapel. At the bottom of our street, before you reached the railway line and the river, was a square of wasteland. On this vacant lot a square brick hut had been built which housed the local cobbler. It was a dark little building with a stable door over which fragile shoes were passed to be resurrected to new life by a hunched, reticent little man with skilful hands, and skin the colour of leather. I thought of him as our resident gnome and was proud that he had chosen the end of our street to inhabit.

The corner shop at the start of our street, a couple of doors above our house, was reminiscent of Arkwright's emporium, Ronnie Barker's shop in "Open all hours".

was owned by an Indian chap and his English wife. Their son and daughter were part of the street's child population unremarkable except for their slightly darker colouring, their exotic names, and their access to an infinite supply of broken biscuits. I remember their back yard always swarmed with wasps in summer time.

The Shop is still there in 2004

Every house had a high walled backyard, at the end of which stood a toilet and a coalhouse. The coalhouses had little hatches that let out onto the back lane. Through these, coal was shovelled from the heaps deposited by the coal man in the back lane. The front streets, as I mentioned, were covered in loose stones, the back lanes, however, were cobbled.

Weeds sprouted here and there between them, just to add a touch of green, and overhead, especially on a Monday, fluttered lines of washing.

Every one dried their washing in the back lane. Sometimes, looking down it at ground level, you saw a forest of wooden clothes props holding up the lines of flapping washing, and you could guarantee that when the props were at their thickest, that would be the day the coal man's horse and cart would come clopping down the street.

"Hey up missis!" he would shout, as housewives rushed to rescue their washing from contamination by his coaly cart. He would deposit gleaming black heaps at each back gate, then go on his way to cause merry havoc down another back lane. The heaps of coal were shovelled safely into the coalhouse and thence by the bucket full onto the living room fire, the only source of heat in the house

"HEY UP MISSIS"

"Hey up missis!" comes the shout
 And the women bustle out.
"Here's the coal man," they all say
"He always comes on washing day!"

Props are lowered, pegs pulled out,
Frantic housewives rush about
Harvesting their washing lines,
Will they get them in on time?

Clipping clopping down the road,
The coal man's horse comes with his load
Oblivious to all the bustle
Steadily, he won't be hustled.

Down The Town

Patiently at every gate
He lowers his dusty head to wait
Sooty sacks the coal man heaves,
Dumps them at the gate and leaves.

Progress through the streets is slow,
The grimy horse just seems to know
Which are gates where he must stop,
As through back lanes he goes, clip clop.

<u>IN DAYS OF OLD…</u>

The Methodist Chapel which occupied the block above our street played an important part in my young life. For one thing whenever there was a wedding at the chapel, gangs of children from the surrounding streets rushed there to hold the bride and groom to ransom until there had been a "hoy oot" —— a shower of small change thrown by the groom as an offering to the children to let him and his bride pass.

The scramble for coins was most undignified, but great fun, and a real windfall in those austere post war years.

Mam was also keen to have her daughter suitably instructed in religion, so I was a regular attender at the Sunday school in the chapel basement. I don't think Mam realised what that Sunday school was like. It consisted of three rows of folding wooden chairs in a bare cement basement, before which a brave but colourless Sunday school teacher intoned texts from the Bible.

Usually, within seconds, some of the boys forced into attendance by diligent mothers, had started a brawl. Chairs were knocked over, sometimes even thrown, it bore more resemblance to a wild west saloon than a Methodist Sunday school!

In spite of this, most children managed to learn their "piece"—— a verse from the Bible, or a poem with religious overtones, to be recited at a great annual event of the chapel, the Sunday School Anniversary. Anticipation of this great event was tremendous in our neighbourhood. It began when each child was handed his or her "piece" to be learned by heart. I bore mine proudly home, and being unable, as yet, to read, was frantic to find out what message the printed words held.

As luck would have it, my father was between shifts, ensconced in a fireside chair in the living room. I homed in on him excitedly and begged him to read my "piece" out loud so that I could learn it by heart, for no one read their "piece" from the paper at the anniversary. Every child was required to stand up at the front of the chapel and recite from memory.

My father took the small scrap of paper in his hand, squinted at it, and solemnly intoned: -

"In days of old
When knights were bold
Before paper was invented
They wiped their bums on cabbage leaves
And went to bed contented."

I listened to him, wide eyed, and consigned the verse to memory, thankful that it was so easy to learn. During the few days preceding the anniversary I rehearsed my "piece" repeatedly in my mind. I was word perfect, and excitedly looking forward to the great day.

When it finally arrived, I was washed, polished, decked in my best frock and a new white ribbon fastened into my hair. On arrival at Sunday school, I was amazed to see the brawling boys looking spick and span —— shoes polished, shirts gleaming and unruly hair flattened by liberal helpings of brylcream.

They shuffled uncomfortably from one foot to the other and were decidedly subdued. When we were all assembled, our Sunday school teacher led us up the stone steps into the chapel, one end of which was raised like a stage. The pews were packed with chapel goers, liberally salted with proud parents. I hadn't bargained for this vast audience.

Somehow, I had assumed that I would recite my "piece" only to the other patrons of the Sunday school. It had never occurred to me that this was to be a performance of such magnitude. I perched nervously on the edge of my allocated seat.

Thankfully, this was near the back of the stage, so I was able to look around and get my bearings without being closely observed. The pipes of the organ reared towards the ceiling behind me. In front of me, past the collection of preening girls and uncomfortable boys, was a sea of faces glowing with anticipation.

Beyond them were the big double doors that led out onto the main road. I fixed my gaze longingly on these, but they were firmly closed. I was trapped!

An old Postcard of Newburn showing the Chapel bottom Right

The proceedings got off to a rousing start with a hymn that nearly lifted the roof, They must have heard us in Newcastle. I enjoyed that, as I love to hear a good song well sung. It saddens me that many of today's children do not know the good old hymns, often singing instead songs of worship which are more akin to jingles.
The hymn concluded, the congregation resumed their seats and a man I'd never seen before began to speak.

He extolled the virtues of Sunday schools in general and this one in particular, and then introduced the first performer.

It was an older girl of about nine years, who rose confidently to her feet, clanked to the front of the stage in noisy new shoes, clasped her hands in front of her, and, gazing piously at the ceiling, regaled the congregation with an epic verse. I can not remember a thing about the subject matter, except that it was in religious vein. I was transfixed with a mixture of admiration and horror. Admiration at the aplomb of the performer, and horror at the thought that soon, it would be my turn. One by one, each child strode or shuffled, according to their confidence, to the front of the stage, and declaimed clearly, or mumbled inaudibly, the verse or text they had learned.

At last, with stark terror, I heard my own name being announced. My mind went blank. The piece about bold knights which I had so diligently learned, fled my brain completely, and I remained rooted to the seat. Again I heard my name called, this time with a note of strain. Had the building been on fire, I could not have moved. Mind empty of anything except fear of having to confront that sea of expectant faces.

The chapel was perfectly still, the atmosphere crackled with tension as my name was called for the third time.

With difficulty, I turned my head and stared, terror stricken, at the man in charge of the proceedings. To my eternal gratitude, he understood immediately.

"Well now, I think we have a touch of stage fright here," he said lightly, and with a conspiratorial smile at the congregation, went on,

"So perhaps young Master. Derek Hogg would like to step forward and speak his piece?"

The congregation smiled at each other, nodded in understanding, then settled back to hear my play mate from down the street mutter the poem which he had mutinously learned. I saw my mother's face displaying disappointment and understanding in equal proportions. I was sorry that I'd let her down.

Years later, when I recalled the verse I was to recite, I felt sure that her slight disappointment was far preferable to the burning shame she would have endured, had I actually stood up in chapel and recited, " In days of old when knights were bold"———

THE SUNDAY SCHOOL ANIVERSARY

At four I was a shy child
Of demeanour very meek.
I went to local Sunday school
At chapel every week.

A great event was coming up
The anniversary "do"
A concert where we all said
Little poems that we knew.

Down The Town

Being Sunday school, these poems
Were of religious bent,
To be an inspiration
To all sinners to repent.

My little piece of paper
With my verse written upon it
I carried home and asked my dad
To read to me the sonnet

He carefully held the paper
And read to me out loud
The piece of verse I would recite
To make my mother proud.

"In days of old, when knights were bold
Before paper was invented
They wiped their bums on cabbage leaves
And went to bed contented."

It never even crossed my mind
To question what he said,
So quickly I consigned the verse
To memory in my head.

The great event at last arrived
The chapel filled up quickly
While backstage, waiting for my turn
I began to feel quite sickly.

Down The Town

I heard the others go on stage
And say their piece with vigour
While butterflies inside my tum
Developed even bigger.

The verse went round inside my head
I went over it and through it
As time grew near for me to speak
I knew I had to do it

"And now for little Lorna's turn"
I heard the compere say
"I'm sure you'll enjoy hearing
What she has got to say"

My feet were rooted to the spot
I couldn't move at all
I heard my name repeated
But just couldn't heed the call.

The concert over, people gone,
The chapel now was quiet
Although, if I'd got up to speak
There would have been a riot.

Years later, when I understood
The verse that I had learned
Relief replaced the previous bout
Of shame with which I'd burned.

Down The Town

My guardian angel must have been
On tenterhooks, or worse
I'm glad he/ she prevented me
From speaking out that verse.

P.S. On a recent visit to Newburn to take a photograph of the chapel for this book, I found that it has been pulled down and replaced by housing.

THAT'S ENTERTAINMENT

One of my playmates, Derek Hogg, lived about six doors down the street. He was the youngest of three children, although his elder brother, Ernest, and big sister, Sheila, were no longer children in my eyes. Indeed I thought of Derek as an only child in a house full of adults, all of whom referred to him as "Our Kidda".

His mam, Lilly, was a cheerful, twinkling brown eyed little woman, full of laughter and kindness, who was a good friend to my mother. His dad, Wilf, was quieter, and the couple began a friendship with my parents which endured long after we moved away from the precipitous street where they lived.

Me (front right) with the Hogg family

It shames me now to admit that, at first, I was afraid of Wilf. I realised later that he was the kindest of men, But, at three years old, his name used to strike terror to my heart. I was well aware of the tribulations brought on Red Riding Hood and the Three Little Pigs

by the Big Bad Wolf, and in my child's mind, "Wilf" became "Wolf".
(Oddly enough in later years I married a man named Wilf – funny
how things work out.)

When I saw him coming down the street, I used to duck into the
house and watch him go by, scanning his slight frame for wolf like
characteristics. As a result of a mining accident, Wilf had lost an eye.
The glass replacement did give him an unusual look, which added to
my conviction that he could, at any moment, change into a wolf and
leap at my throat. All this, mark you, before I had ever heard of
werewolves! It just shows how fertile a child's imagination can be.

Derek was a little younger than me, a lively brown-eyed boy, the
image of his mam. Like all boys then, he wore "Lang short uns"———
— short trousers which hovered just above the knee. The lower part
of his legs was supposed to be covered by knee socks, but Derek's
knee socks showed a complete inability to defy gravity, and invariably
slid gracefully down to nestle comfortably around his ankles. His
exposed shins and knees displayed scratches, bruises and grazes in
varying stages of recovery.

Sticking plasters were unheard of and bandages were a luxury kept
only for the most severe of injuries. My own knees usually bore a
battle scar or two, as stone strewn and cobbled streets are not the
safest of landing places.

We didn't always play in the streets of course. Often we would hole
in to someone's back yard, where we could play in perfect safety,
watched from the scullery window by a benevolent mother.

Back yards were magic. To the casual observer they appeared expanses of bare concrete, bounded by high brick walls, sometimes topped with broken glass. But, with a little imagination, they could be transformed into the wild west, treasure island, a smuggler's cave, or anything else the heart desired.

One little girl down our street regularly transformed her back yard in a more tangible way. Her name was Shirley. I'm not sure whether she was inspired by Shirley Temple films at our local "flea pit" or her stage debut at the Sunday school anniversary, but Shirley went in for show business in a big way.

The out side toilet served as her dressing room. Her mother's clothes line was diverted to hang across the yard —— draped with dustsheets, it made a splendid curtain. Rows of kitchen chairs and stools borrowed from Shirley's mam and the houses on either side, were set with their backs to the scullery door.

It is hard to describe the air of mystery bestowed on that back yard by a single clothes line and a couple of dust sheets, but the aura was such that every child, once inside the back yard gate, crept to their seats and sat, hushed and expectant.

The air was thick with suppressed excitement and when the dust sheets were finally hauled aside to reveal a blonde ringleted Shirley against a backdrop of outside toilet and coal house doors, the sharp intake of breath just about sucked all the oxygen out of the street!

The Entertainer

The actual performance, (a few songs and dances I think) has not imprinted itself upon my memory. What has remained is the anticipation, excitement and sheer air of theatre this little girl was able to create. I hope she has happy memories of those back yard concerts. I know I have.

Another person with a theatrical bent was the wife of the local police sergeant. (A lady who greatly impressed my mother by having two different kinds of sauce on her table) She and her two equally extrovert daughters were wont to throw impromptu concerts on the steps of the war memorial. ("I'm a sopriano you know." She boasted to my mam.)

Life was seldom dull in those days!

Newburn War Memorial

Sometimes, as a treat, mam would take Linda in her pram, with me skipping alongside, for a walk to Throckly dene. This was a wooded cleft in the landscape on the edge of our neighbouring village and was no mean walk for a four year old, but I loved it.

A trickle of water bubbled through it and the wooded banks were awash with bluebells in spring and early summer. The main road west from Newcastle went past its entrance and I remember one very special day, we emerged from our stroll through its leafy pathways to find the main road fringed with excited people.

It transpired that Princess Margaret was expected to pass by at any moment. Goodness knows where she had been, or indeed, where she was going, but the opportunity to see a real princess was not to be missed

We hadn't long to wait. Cheers rippled along the road as the large, shiny black car drew nearer. It travelled very slowly, so we had a perfect view of an extremely pretty girl, face aglow, dressed all in pink and looking exactly as I had imagined a princess should. She was waving happily. I can't help comparing this memory of her then with the last time she was seen in public. Life has a way of changing us all.

On the way home, we called at the baby clinic to pick up a tin of the "National Dried" milk on which my baby sister was fed. The woman in charge fussed over Linda as she was weighed etc. They kept a close check on her because of her premature birth, but she seemed to be doing quite nicely. Mam and dad often exchanged smiles over the self importance of one of the clinic ladies, who had once assured my bemused father that,

"All the milk in Newburn comes through me!"

FURTHER AFIELD.

As the children of Davison street grew a little older, our horizons widened, and we discovered an exciting world beyond. First we were allowed down the hill, where a street parallel to the river headed west, past the football ground, towards a shallow, sandy banked burn where we could plodge about to our hearts content, frocks tucked into knickers, catching tiddlers with nets made from our mams old stockings, and depositing them in jam jars with string handles.

Down by the river --

-- with man

-- and with Dad.

Sometimes, we took a picnic of bread and butter and a pop bottle full of water. Occasionally we had a hard boiled egg as a special treat. The empty pop bottle was always carried safely home afterwards so that it could be returned to the shop in exchange for a few precious pennies. An efficient form of recycling, I wonder why they don't do it now?

If we followed the street in an easterly direction towards Newburn bridge instead, it took us past the Co-op, various small shops and, on the opposite side of the road, Eddie Liddle's piggery, to the Mecca for us children, the cinema and neighbouring ice cream parlour.

"The pictures," as the cinema was known, was sheer heaven. Every Saturday afternoon there was a matinee performance. It was well worth the mayhem of a cinema full of unruly kids to savour the adventures of Hopalong Cassidy, Roy Rodgers and my particular favourite, Gene Autry. I still love a good western, probably because they were my first cinematic experience.

Newburn Cinema as it is today

Comedies were popular too —— "Fatty and Skinny" as Laurel and Hardy were commonly known, and later, the Three Stooges. I have vague memories of the Marx brothers as well. Harpo was the only one worth a light in my book. I thought the others were too silly for words, but Harpo had REAL talent — he was musical. Tears would spring to my eyes when he played.

I suffered the ridiculous antics of his brothers, waiting for the section in the film when the whistling, curly haired buffoon would take up his harp and transport me to paradise!

I clearly remember my annoyance at being socked in the back of the neck by someone's boot one Saturday, just at the point when Harpo was beginning to play. (Hurling footwear was a popular pass-time at Saturday matinees)

Next to "the pictures" was Mark Tony's ice cream parlour.
To sit in one of its booths enjoying delicious ice cream was considered the height of sophistication.

Another attractive shop near "the pictures" belonged to Derek's aunt Edna and uncle John. It was a veritable Aladdin's cave, since it sold all manner of confectionery AND toys.

Wherever he went in Newburn, Derek was never far from his family. His Mam's sister and her husband ran the aforementioned shop, his maternal grandmother lived on the opposite side of our street and other relatives seemed to be liberally sprinkled about the district. I used to envy him, his family were so accessible and often together in large friendly gatherings.

My grandparents, aunts and uncles seemed so far away ———— no more weekly visits to my South Shields nana, and the journey to my country grandparents was so difficult, that I rarely saw them, (apart from my annual summer holiday there).

Occasionally, aunty Elsie, one of mam's two youngest sisters (twins, Elsie and Eva) would trek over from South Shields, usually bearing an exotic gift such as a dollop of cod's roe or even better, a pint of prawns, but these pleasant visits were infrequent.

Derek's happy family always made me welcome and enfolded me to their collective bosom, which did much to fill the gap. It was through frequent visits to Derek's home that I began to realise that his father, Wilf, was not at all fearsome. In fact, I discovered, he was a lovely man with a quiet sense of humour, the perfect foil for his ebullient twinkling eyed little wife.

It was in Derek's home at one of these family gatherings that I endured a meal of excruciating torment. Mam, dad and I had been invited to join the family for Sunday tea. Unfortunately, this came only days after I had realised that whenever I ate anything, the most appalling noise ensued. Keeping my mouth clamped shut seemed to do nothing to diminish the row, and I was sure that anyone in my vicinity must be deafened by what sounded to me like a gravel crusher working flat out. Watching closely while my parents ate their meals I observed that, not a sound escaped from between their lips. I concluded that there must be something vital missing from my mouth. Sound proofing perhaps?

Lilly had excelled herself. The spread set out before us was mouth watering. From my seat next to Derek on the wooden form I peered over the edge of the table at the array of home made pies, scones, cakes and trifles. Wondering what would make the least noise, I selected a cheese scone, oozing butter. Taking a small bite, I began, slowly and carefully to chew it. It was no use, the noise was incredible. I scanned the faces round the table anxiously. No one seemed to have noticed, they were all cheerfully eating, laughing and chatting as though they couldn't hear the deafening din.

I decided that they were just being tactful. It seemed ages before I had the mouthful of scone in a fit state to swallow, then, looking at the rest of the scone on my plate, I wondered how on earth to dispose of it.

Inspiration struck suddenly, my knicker leg! Knicker legs, which came much further down the leg in those days, were the great universal pocket. Some posh knickers actually had real pockets sewn into them, but most just had tight elastic round the leg, under which hankies, sweeties and any other treasure was tucked. Clutching the remains of the scone, I sat demurely, hands in my lap. Furtively, I hiked up my frock at one side and tucked the remains of the scone under my knicker elastic. Glancing around, I was relieved to see that this delicate manoeuvre had not been observed.

Next, I selected a piece of sponge cake, but with the same noisy result when I began to chew, so, it joined the scone and I gave up. I was sorry to forgo the pleasures of Lilly's home cooking, but my embarrassment at the noisy mechanics of chewing far outweighed my greed. I would especially have liked some trifle, but didn't dare risk having to transfer that to my knicker leg. I went home famished and with my knicker legs full of crumbs.

It was weeks before I confided my worry to my mother and was reassured that everyone could hear the sound of their own chewing, but with the mouth closed, no one else could hear a thing. What a relief!

Other members of the family seemed to have no such constraints about eating. My cousin Betty, for instance, once ate someone's gold watch! She was only a baby at the time, but nevertheless, it seemed to be taking a "wide and varied diet" a little too far.

The owner of the watch, great aunt Janet I think, (see "Up the Valley") had insisted upon its return, so everyone waited for Betty to pass the time!

A MIXED UP INFANT

Carefree days of playing in the street and back yards were soon to end. At the other side of the main road lay a building the existence of which I was blissfully ignorant, Newburn primary school.

In the normal course of events, I would not have crossed its portals until the age of five. However, my mother, in the mistaken belief that it would be a good move to keep me off the streets, harassed the authorities until they allowed me to start school early.

Now the streets of Newburn, by any standards were pretty innocuous, but to my anxious mother, whose view was coloured by the profession of my father, these apparently peaceful streets were full of hooligans and fraught with danger.

School was a real shock to my system. The teacher was a tall thin, stern faced spinster who presided over the class with an imperious manner. I detected no sign of sympathy in her for my plight. Worse, I knew no one in the class.

At nine am, when the teacher rang the bell, we ran to stand in rigid lines in the yard, before marching into the various classrooms arranged around the central hall. The high windows in these rooms were situated to give light, but not view. The walls were painted puke green and the pipes and radiators were a darker shade of the same colour.

The desks, with seats attached to them, were lined up across the classroom in precise order facing the one teaching aid in the room the blackboard. Our mentor was seated at a tall desk to one side of the board. If she left her seat the class cowered, for our teacher on the prowl was a fearsome creature, apt to rap errant knuckles with a ruler, or, if really provoked, skelp the culprit round the ear.

I was mystified by the whole set up, which was such a contrast to my former carefree existence. On one terrifying occasion I inadvertently lined up in the yard with the wrong class. This may sound a stupid thing to do, but in the mass of bodies surging and pushing to get into line before "Miss" lost patience, I was simply pulled along with the flow.

Once in position, I daren't change, for in that regimented array of children standing smartly to attention, any movement would undoubtedly attract the unwelcome attention of the teacher wielding the bell. Rather than incur her anger, I stood stock still in the line and duly followed it into a strange classroom.

The class of older children to which I had become attached, strode confidently to their desks and sat down. I spotted a vacant seat next to a girl right in the front and slid gratefully into it, hoping to remain unnoticed until the next recess.

I might have managed it too, if it hadn't been for a blasted wasp! This unwelcome visitor flew in about half way through the lesson and caused a minor panic among the children immediately behind me, thus drawing the teacher's attention to that area of the room. I sank lower in my seat, but it was no good, I'd been spotted. Her eyebrows shot up, her finger shot out and her bellow of outrage reverberated round the room.

"WHAT," she demanded to know, "ARE YOU DOING HERE?"

The wasp was forgotten as all eyes focussed on me.

The Wasp

Those sitting near, who had been giving me curious glances now allowed themselves unabashed stares, even a few derisive sniggers.

Fear froze my vocal chords, and, unable to answer, I was hauled from the seat by my collar. I had no idea what to expect next.

Summary execution would not have surprised me.

However, after her initial shock at finding a mixed infant of the wrong variety in her class, the teacher merely delegated a big girl to escort me back to my own room, where I slunk, red faced, to my rightful seat at the back.

Throughout my school career I was always allocated a seat at the back because of being tall for my age. This was a mixed blessing. For a shy child, it had its advantages, but in later years, when my sight suddenly deteriorated, (a condition I was determined to conceal,) copying from the blackboard became impossible, so I had to throw myself on the mercy of my neighbours and copy at second hand from their books.

Apart from straying into the wrong classroom, the only other memories of my first school are, the ease with which I learned to read, a delivery of apples, and my dread of maths lessons.

The apples were a gift from the people of Canada. I well remember the excitement in those post war years of rationing, when the whole school was marshalled in the hall and each child was given two huge rosy apples. We were so stunned by this unexpected windfall, that we accepted them in grateful silence.

I have been favourably disposed towards Canadians ever since.

A less favourable impression was made by my earliest maths lessons. It was a requirement of our teacher that, when practising numbers on our slates, we write the figure three in the flat topped variety.

Try as I might, I could not master it. My feeble efforts so infuriated my teacher that she eventually began every maths lesson by writing a huge three on the board and bellowing, as she dragged me by the ear, red faced and mortified, to the front of the class,

"THAT IS FOR THE BENEFIT OF LORNA NAIRN, WHO STILL CANNOT WRITE A THREE!!!"

Though my early efforts at maths fell short of the mark, I did excel in reading. Newburn mixed infants didn't read books. We read cards which bore a sepia tinted picture at the top and a few lines of print underneath. The cards were much thumbed and very grubby.

However, unattractive as these teaching aids were, I took to reading like a duck to water. My moment of glory came when I was sent across the hall to the head teacher's office to display my prowess to this oracle, and I returned to the classroom glowing with pride.

I could not for the life of me understand why the school declared itself to be for "mixed infants." This conjured up for me a picture of variegated children, rather like sweets in a packet of dolly mixtures and, as far as I could see, apart from some of us being boys, and some, girls, we were all pretty much the same.

Boys and girls were not allowed to mix anyway. In class we never sat together and at play time we had separate yards which even had a high wall between them! Perhaps it should have said "mixed up infants," if my experience is anything to go by.

THE LESSON LEARNED

When I was very little
At the early age of four
I went into a building
That I'd never seen before.

Down The Town

It said it housed mixed infants
On the sign above the gate,
I crossed its gloomy portals
Resigned to my sad fate.

The infants there were very mixed
Some naughty, some quite good,
Some boys, some girls, some short, some tall,
Some sad or happy mood.

We all learned how to stand in line
And how to sit quite still,
I learned to read, but how to write?
Did not quite fit the bill.

The figure three defeated me,
And so I lived in fear
Of Miss's pounce and screamed tirade,
The pulling on my ear.

The lesson that I learned from this
Served me in later years,
That children need encouragement
And seldom learn through fear.

HOSPITAL

School was not my first encounter with a large institution. Soon after I turned four, I was taken by my mother to a forbidding looking building down the town and abandoned

I remember standing by the side of a high metal bed in a ward full of similar beds, wondering what I was doing there. A nurse briskly told me to undress and put on the hospital gown, before stamping off confidently to another area of her domain. Obediently, I stripped off to my vest and liberty bodice, and looked around for the aforementioned hospital gown——nothing. I looked under the bed, in the small locker beside it, under the pillow—- no gown. I tried to look under the blankets, but they were wrapped around the hard mattress like a bandage, so I wasn't able to prize them up far enough to see whether the elusive gown was hidden there or not. The ward wasn't very warm. Wrapping my arms around myself, I stood, semi-naked, like a concentration camp victim, awaiting my unknown fate.

It seemed like a very long time before the stamping figure of authority returned. No "angel of mercy" this, she was furious.

"Why aren't you in bed? You haven't even got your gown on yet." She bellowed. Terrified, I managed to communicate the absence of said gown to this harridan, and off she stamped again in search of the missing item. Eventually, she returned, tight lipped with frustration, bearing a large liberty bodice.

I gathered that the supply of regulation gowns had temporarily dried up, and I was to wear the liberty bodice as a substitute. It crossed my mind that, if I had to wear such a garment, my own was as good as any.

Argument seemed inadvisable though, so, obediently, I stripped off my own warm liberty bodice and donned the hospital cold one. It was similar to my own in every respect——— a sleeveless, round necked undergarment, resplendent with rubber buttons. My own ended at about hip level. This larger one came slightly lower, but not low enough to cover my embarrassment. I clambered hastily onto the bed and clawed franticly at the unyielding blankets.

Hospital

With relief, I managed to insinuate myself between the freezing starched sheets and slid down until only my nose and eyes showed. I was aware of children in the other beds, but none of them spoke. Even if they had, I was too paralysed with cold and fear to have answered them. The angry nurse stamped back and forth a few times, but no one else came near until the food was dished out.

My appetite, normally healthy, had fled.

However, I did as I was told and ate the meal.

The drink though, was another matter, it was Bovril, which I hated and so, left. I had, however, bargained without our stamping friend.

Her eyebrows shot up, her hand shot out, and she shoved the offending drink under my nose. The smell of it was enough to make me feel sick, but the nurse was not to be balked.

"Get this drink down you NOW."
She ordered. My protestations were stifled by luke warm Bovril as she forced the cup to my lips. No sooner was the drink down than it made the return journey, all over the starched sheets and the starched nurse. She was not amused. She and her cohorts were, however, stubborn, so, at every meal I was made to drink Bovril, which I immediately and involuntarily deposited back in their laps.

The whole dreadful experience was climaxed by a miserable awakening from what I now know was the removal of my tonsils and adenoids. All I knew at the time was that I had a very sore throat, and felt sick. Unfortunately, I was, all over the starched nurse. I must confess to a certain satisfaction at my aim, despite my discomfort.

The worst part of the whole thing was the growing conviction that I had been abandoned by my parents and would spend the rest of my life here in this awful place with the stamping, starched wardress.

It says much for the adaptability of children, that I was resigned to my fate. A deep sadness settled on me, but it never occurred to me to rebel. Maybe I was just a wimp!

This minor ordeal was but a paltry blip in my life, compared to what some children have to endure. Now, reading newspaper accounts of the tortured existence of yet another mistreated child, reminds me of that short, unhappy spell in hospital.

The distress I suffered was negligible, not inflicted deliberately and in no way compares to the ordeals endured by some unfortunate children, but it gave me a glimmer of insight into the helpless despair some children are forced to live with. I am grateful that my experience was so minor and so short lived

After a few days of enforced Bovril and (of all things for a sore throat), toast, I was suddenly dressed in my own clothes and taken into another room. Here there were toys— jigsaws, teddy bears, even a rocky horse, and a few other children, looking equally as mystified.

Even more surprising, we were each given a bowl of jelly and ice cream, sheer bliss on our sore throats. I was still trying to make sense of all this, when, to my astonishment, across the room, I saw my mother. Relief! I was going HOME

SEATON BURN.

Home was not to be in our tilted terraced house for much longer. I would be about five and a half when the exciting news came that we were to move to a police house in Seaton Burn, a mining village which was "a single station."

In effect, this meant that the police station was incorporated into the house, including official telephone and police cells. It also meant that the Police service gained an unpaid workforce, the policemen's wives, who manned the phones and single stations when their husbands were out on duty.

I can't speak for all police wives, but I know that, throughout his career, my mother did almost as much police work as my father, for no financial reward, or even acknowledgement of her vital role.

The most exciting attributes of our new home, however, weren't the two cells, but the long strip of garden at the front and an area of rough grass outside our back yard gate. Whiskey, our cat, was ecstatic, and so was I. It was almost as good as being in the country.

The fact that we stepped out of our garden gate straight onto the Great North Road, (the A.1.) was neither here nor there. (The short terrace of three houses, of which the police house was the centre, have since been demolished and the Seaton Burn Working Men's Club has expanded to cover where it once stood.)

Like our previous home, this one had no electricity, illumination being provided by gas lights which hung from the centre of the ceiling in the front room (which doubled as the police office) and the living room. In the scullery, the gas lights were at the end of metal arms that protruded from the wall. Also in the scullery was the set pot, a large squat brick built edifice containing a fire in the base, on which to heat water for washing day.

In those days before the advent of the washing machine, doing the laundry involved carrying buckets of water to the set pot to be heated, pounding the dirty clothes in a tub with a poss stick, then passing the whole lot between the rollers of a mangle. This could cause havoc with buttons, which often emerged in pieces. It didn't do much for fingers either!

Through the scullery, (and actually indoors) was the lavatory, beyond that were the two cells. They each contained a lavatory and a hard wooden bed. They were absolutely freezing, so in the absence of a refrigerator, it was Mam's habit to use one of the cells to set jellies and trifles for Sunday lunch time. This was fine, until one Saturday night, Dad locked up a recalcitrant drunk, who emerged, sober and replete on Sunday morning.

The other use to which one of the cells was put, was to provide a safe haven where our newly acquired tortoise, Toby, could hibernate. Good job Toby wasn't in residence at the same time as the hungry drunk, he might have mistaken our tortoise for a rather tough pasty!

Toby was a much loved addition to our family, so when he went missing one summer day, we were extremely distressed. This gave way to incredulous amusement when he turned up along the street in the bar of the local working men's club.

We had to suffer endless jokes about his tremendous thirst, his lack of a membership card, his amorous designs on the pork pies etc., but it was worth it to have him back.

For the first few weeks at Seaton Burn, I was a little home sick, so to help me over this Mam invited one of my Newburn friends, Sylvia to stay. We spent a happy day while I showed her round my new domain, and at night we snuggled together in the same bed chatting and giggling until late at night. Next morning, I approached Mam with a question which had been puzzling me.

"Mam, you know when we are standing up, Sylvia is much smaller than me?"

"Yes. Answered Mam, uncertain what was coming next.

" Well, how come when we are lying in bed we are the same height?"

I never did get a satisfactory answer. Mam was too busy laughing.

Me (on the right), Linda and friends at Seaton Burn

Our neighbours were mainly miners, who worked in the local pit, so it was a common sight to see men blackened from head to foot in coal dust wending their way wearily home at the end of each shift. Pit-head baths were a thing of the future. My new playmates were the children of these men.

I particularly remember Ken Gibson, Ian Story, Ann Bennett and Elizabeth Hunter, amongst others. We had wonderful times, building ramshackle tree houses in a nearby overgrown hawthorn hedge. It must have been an eye sore to the local residents, so it says a lot for their tolerance that it was allowed to remain.

Another favourite summer pastime was walking to "The Big Waters," or, more accurately, a small stream which fed into it. Here we played happily for hours catching tadpoles and tiddlers, (stickle backs) with home made stocking nets. Summer evenings were spent happily playing in the streets.

Usually our games were harmless, like hide and seek or hop scotch, but occasionally we played " knocky nine doors", or a variation of this where we tied two adjacent doors together, then knocked on them and stood back to watch the tussle.

Rationing was still in force, so sweets were doled out with care. When coupons (and cash) were available, we children clustered into Watson's confectionery shop, a couple of doors from the club and bought sherbet dabs, liquorice root, or aniseed balls.

On the opposite side of the main road were the doctor's the undertaker's and the church. (A convenient arrangement I suppose).

The undertaker, Lance Hood, lived with his wife, Ethel above the workshop where he made beautiful coffins, lined with satin, mainly white but occasionally pale blue, pink or mauve. Their upstairs accommodation was most genteel. Linda and I were impressed by the number of lace doilies festooning the place, absolutely everything stood on its own lace doily, but Ethel's carefully cultivated air of gentility could slip on occasion.

Like the time father popped in for a cup of tea one day, and, having drained his cup, noticed that it was cracked. Teasingly, he drew this to Ethel's attention.

"Oh don't worry about that Bob," she declared airily, "That's just the cup I use to steep my teeth in".

Dad and Mr. Hood became great pals, a happy state of affairs for me, as I fell heir to all the off cuts of beautiful material. I must have had the only dolls in the country who were dressed in shrouds!

Come to think of it, it was about that time that mam made Linda and I the most beautiful matching dresses with puffed sleeves, gathered skirts and embroidered with little rosebuds. The material was satin of a fetching shade of mauve. Perhaps it wasn't only our dolls who were bedecked in shrouds! I do know that Linda and I were immensely proud of our pretty dresses, our usual attire being more often hand-me-downs from older cousins.

My father, being an agnostic, did not have a lot of time for men of the cloth. The local vicar, Father Williams, though, was an exception to this rule. It may have been because, at six foot four, he was one of the few people who could look Dad in the eye. He had a big personality too, so it wasn't long before the two were on terms of, if not friendship, at least respectful truce.

Dad used to tease him about his apparent ambition to fill up the rambling old vicarage, as Mrs Williams presented him with yet another new son or daughter. I don't know whether it was as a result of this mutual respect or not, but soon after moving to Seaton Burn, our allegiance was transferred from the Methodist chapel to the Church Of England across the road, where the imposing figure of Father Williams held sway.

This was an entirely different form of worship to which I had been used. The church was ornately decorated, as were Father William's robes. The service was extremely "high church", including the use of incense and tinkling bells at intervals, in fact, it seemed to be Catholic in everything but the Pope. I couldn't understand most of it at first, but I loved the beauty of the service and remained a member of this church until we moved away from the area, some years later.

When the time came for me to be confirmed, Father Williams held classes at the vicarage in the preceding weeks. At the end of the course of classes, it was impressed upon us confirmation candidates, that in order to be eligible, we must be in "a state of grace." To achieve this happy state, we must confess all our sins at a special session at church the following week.

Seeing our blank looks, (confession not being a regular feature of our church) Father Williams pointed out a list on the back pages of our "Preparation for Confirmation" handbooks. There, every sin known to man was listed, murder, robbery, rape, the lot.

Diligently, I copied them all out and when it was my turn to make my confession, read out the whole list! Father Williams's shoulders shook a bit, but to his credit, he managed to absolve me without breaking down.

Down The Town

The other important building on the same side as the doctor, undertaker and church, was the Co operative store. Mam got the majority of our groceries here. Most things were sold loose, so our sugar was dolloped into blue bags, the required amount of butter was cut off a big block and wrapped in grease proof paper and bacon was sawed from huge sides by a lethal looking bacon slicer.

The other vital commodity to be had from the Coop was the accumulator, an item without which, the wireless would not work.

This was a large battery which had to be replaced at regular intervals, so it became my task to take the empty one back and bring the heavy new one home, a fact which I have always blamed for my long arms!

It was worth it though, I loved listening to the likes of Jimmy Edwards and "the Glums" also "Ray's a laugh" with Ted Ray and Bebe Daniels and Ben Lyon in "Life with the Lyons"

Above the Co-op was the store hall, a place I was introduced to soon after we moved to Seaton Burn.

The first day at my new school, (long since demolished) gave my teacher something of a problem———- rehearsals were well under way for a school concert which was to be put on in the store hall.

All the parts had been given out, thank goodness, but Miss Nixon was determined to include me in the proceedings, so there was no escape.

I was kitted out with crepe paper costumes and took part in a minuet, a polka and a finale which included loud renditions of "Keep your sunny side up" and "The sun has got his hat on."

The concert was a roaring success and must have done much to brighten the lives of its audience in those days before T.V. but the whole thing was an excruciating experience for me and confirmed what the Sunday School Anniversary had suggested, that I was not a born performer.

THE CORONATION.

The concert apart, Seaton Burn school holds mostly happy memories for me. (Unfortunately, it has long since been demolished.)

The children were friendly, apart from one rather spiteful girl who laughingly informed me that when I smiled I had a chin like a witch. That accounts for my po-faced expression on the school photographs, I was self conscious about smiling for years.

The teachers were pleasant, in the main, and although classes were large and teaching aids were unheard of then, except for the blackboard, and in the older classes, a map of the world, lessons were interesting and instructive.

This lack of equipment, (even the few books had to be shared) meant that when we did get something new, it was very much appreciated.

I remember with pleasure the day we were first given colours to use in illustrating our books. The excitement was tremendous. I must have been about nine at the time.

As I remember, in the youngest classes, we didn't write in books at all, we had small blackboards or slates on which we wrote with chalk!

Seaton Burn Infants 1950

Back Row Left to Right
Frank Bennet Stanley Hogg Lesley Ashurst Josie Platton Eileen Hancocks Jennifer Ball Muriel Marshall Ruth Wilson Jack Wilson Unknown
Second Back Row
Jim Warren Lewis Weaver Mary Smith Elizabeth Hunter **Lorna Nairn** Jean Rutter Gladys Gibson Valerie Turnbull Valerie Hay Valerie Calvert George Calvert
Mervyn Willey
Third Row
Gertrude Lawrence Yvonne Strachan Margaret Dunn Sheila Wilson Ann Reid Joy Lamb John Dinning Sheila Robson Ann Grieves Sandra Legg Jennifer Dodds
Esther Brown Jean Mordue *(with slate board)*
Front Row
Brian Gibbs Colin Bennet Bruce Tinsley Robert Webster Jack Denham Jim Cleugh John Nichol Gordon Walker

In Miss Temperly's class, we were required to make a collection of wild flowers, press them and present the collection, neatly labelled, in an exercise book. We then did the same thing with the leaves of trees. I don't know about all of my class mates, but my friends and I spent happy hours making our collections in the surrounding countryside and I can still recognise and name most of our native trees and wild flowers.

Miss Temperly was also responsible for my first experience of gardening. The caretaker, Mr. Amos, lived in a large grey stone house next door to the school and he gave over the land at the front of the house to Miss Temperly to use as a teaching aid. There, successive classes of eight year olds were instructed in the lore of the garden. As a result, Mr. Amos's front garden would have done credit to any municipal park, with its regimented ranks of alyssum, lobelia, and french marigolds, so fashionable at the time.

Another clear memory concerns the day when an era ended. We children were as usual, sitting silently at our work, when a teacher from another class, came into the room with a strange expression on his face and asked our teacher to step outside for a moment. We looked at each other in amazement, such a thing had never happened before.

We began to speculate, in whispers, then in louder voices, when the door opened and our teacher came back looking rather shaken. We knew that something momentous must have happened, because she didn't tell us off for making a noise, but none of us were prepared for the news she delivered in hushed tones.

"Children, I am very sorry to tell you that King George has died."

It may seem strange, but we were all genuinely sad to hear of the king's death. None of us had even seen him, apart from the occasional newspaper picture, yet we were stunned by the news, as though we had lost a family member.

Our sorrow at the loss of the king was, however, modified somewhat by the realisation that we were to have a new, young queen. The whole idea of having a queen, instead of a king seemed new and exciting. The very word "queen" was strange on the lips. I was thrilled to find that I shared the same middle name as our new monarch and it wasn't long before we all began to look forward to her coronation and the dawning of a new age.

Television had been around for some time before the coronation, but not in the homes of many ordinary people. Most of us had to wait until the film of the great event came to a cinema in our nearest town. For the children of upper Coquetdale, where I spent my summers, this meant a long journey to Newcastle, on a specially hired bus. It was a great day out for them and my cousin, Alan had, apparently, been hugely impressed by the golden coronation coach.

"Bye, that would make a grand mucking out cart!" He had declared to the hushed cinema audience.

Seaton Burn rose to the occasion magnificently. There was a huge tea party at the "miner's welfare" and every child was given a souvenir china mug. I still have mine.

There did exist the odd private television set, but at the time of the coronation they were thin on the ground in our area. However, I do remember the first time I saw a T.V set. It was around the time of the coronation I think. Newcastle United had made it to the cup final at Wembley, a not uncommon event in those days – Newcastle won the Cup three times between 1951 and 1955.

Our neighbour was, in common with the majority of the population, an avid supporter, and though he hadn't a ticket for the match, he had the next best thing——- a relative with a T.V.

Consequently, he and a small group of friends, together with their children, and me, (goodness knows why I was included) set off on the walk to Dinnington village, where the T.V. owner lived.

By the time the Seaton Burn contingent got there, the house was stowed out with men, women and children, all desperate to have a look at this phenomenon, and, if possible view the match.

The house walls were positively bulging, so, I contented myself with a glimpse of its tiny black and white screen, viewed between dozens of heads all staining in its direction. Not much cop, I decided. I much preferred the big screen at our nearest cinema in Wideopen, and spent the entire duration of the match playing in the garden with some of the other children who were not prepared to battle for such a disappointing view. (By the way, Newcastle won.)

One of the advantages of living at Seaton Burn was its relative proximity to the coast. Occasionally, mam and some of the neighbours would take a group of children to Seaton Sluice for a day at the beach. We kids were a motley crew on the beach.

Money was in short supply so not everyone had a bathing costume. I did though! My mother made me one out of scraps of wool which she diligently knitted. I don't think there were more than two lines of the same colour, a veritable woollen rainbow. I was delighted with it, until I went into the sea! The weight of the water stretched my costume, dragging it down till it was round my ankles. Mam had to rescue me with a towel. One of my friends had a costume which her mam had made out of pink lint, but she had the sense to stay out of the water with hers.

Once we even went to Whitley Bay, which was more difficult to get to, because it involved two bus journeys. We had made the special effort, because a bus full of children (and their parents) were coming for the day from Coquetdale on their summer "trip," so mam had arranged to meet auntie Peg and her family, spend the day at the beach with them, then despatch me off with them back to the Coquet valley afterwards.

Whitley Bay was quite a holiday resort then, with its beautiful beaches, complete with beach huts, deck chairs, donkey rides, Punch and Judy shows, not to mention the wonderful array of shops, and the fairground at the "Spanish City."

We met auntie Peg and the Coquet contingent off their bus and headed for the beach. We children were in high spirits, all except my cousin, Alan. It had been a long journey confined on the bus and he was desperate to "spend a penny."

"Hout, ye'll just hetta wait till ye get to the sea," said Peg. "we're nearly there."

"I'm no' gannin in the sea," retorted Alan indignantly. "ha' they not got netties here?"

"Don't worry Alan we'll pass some public toilets soon," said mam, "in fact there they are, just over there."
Alan took off, and before anyone could stop him, vanished into the ladies toilet.

"What do yee think yer playin at gannin in there?" asked an amused auntie Peg when he emerged.

Quite unabashed, Alan replied "Well, it says "laddies ower the door."

'Laddies' Toilet

Needless to say, a good time was had by all, and at the end of the day,

I joined auntie Peg and her family to spend a few carefree weeks up the Coquet valley.

SHANDY.

When nana and granda moved away from Coquetdale, I had two venues for my summer breaks—— I still went up the valley with auntie Peg, but also visited nana and granda in whichever part of Northumberland they happened to be living at the time. One year, it was a tiny cottage on the coast opposite the Holy Island of Lindisfarne, where, as well as the usual animals for company, I made friends with the taxi drivers who drove people over the sand to the island when the tides were right.

There was no causeway to the island in those days. Once, one of the drivers took granda and I for a free trip. It was most intriguing to set off across the wide stretch of wet sand which separated Holy Island from the mainland. The bottom edges of the old cars were all rusty— I soon discovered why. At one point there appeared to be the equivalent of a burst water main in the bottom of the car! Granda also took me with him on a trip into Berwick one day and treated me to a quarter of Berwick cockles, the town's trade mark confection. Delicious!

The fields where Granda 'looked' his sheep here were much tamer than those up the Coquet Valley but I did enjoy accompanying him occasionally. Once we found a tiny leveret crouched in the grass waiting for the mother hare to return. We left it there and steered the dogs away from the area to keep it safe.

On that particular visit, nana's little ginger cat (daughter of my old favourite, Dante, see "Up the Valley") had produced a litter of kittens which she had managed, with my help, to rear to an age when they were safe from granda's cull.

One of them was the most gorgeous little ginger tom, so I was desperate to keep him. I didn't think my chances were very good, because we already had Whisky, our grey cat, but I decided to give it a try. On a scrap of paper, with a stub of pencil, I wrote the following ill spelt note.

"deer mamey pleez can I hav a citn he is jinja and his nam is shandy."

To my absolute astonishment, the answer was "yes", so when mam came to collect me to take me home, Shandy, the ginger kitten accompanied us, fastened up in an old shopping bag. He was a character from the start and soon charmed not only our family, including Whisky, but most of the neighbours as well. He had an especially close relationship with Rachael, an older lady who lived alone in a tiny two roomed house just around the corner. We didn't mind sharing his affections with her—— he always came home after his visits, until one memorable sunny day.

I had been playing out late in the balmy summer evening, but knew something was amiss as soon as I came through the door. The air of tension in the house was palpable, mam looked worried, Linda was crying and dad was in the sort of volatile mood which always descended on him when things weren't going his way.

"What's the matter?" I asked cautiously.
"Shandy's gone missing." whispered mam. That explained father's temper, he adored Shandy.

"I'll go and look round the allotments," I said and rushed out, glad to be away from father's vicinity. He could be unpredictable and scarey when in a bad mood. Shandy could often be seen sunning himself in the allotments out the back of our house.

Dad had one of them, where he grew vegetables and kept half a dozen handsome black and white speckled hens. Perhaps Shandy was there. He wasn't.

We didn't find him at all that evening. I lay awake for as long as I could that night, hoping to hear him meowing at the back door. Nothing. With heavy heart I went to school next day, hoping that Shandy would have turned up by the time I came home. He hadn't. Next day was Saturday, but it seemed to stretch emptily ahead without Shandy's presence. In the early afternoon our worst fears were confirmed. Dad came home carrying Shandy's beautiful golden body. He looked perfect, but he was quite dead.

" Hit by a car on the Dudley road." muttered dad.

He got the spade and dug a hole in Shandy's favourite sunny corner of the garden. Mam lined a cardboard box with some of Mr. Hood's left over shroud material. The rich ginger fur looked lovely against the pale blue satin, We buried him with as much ceremony as we could muster, Linda and I silently weeping, then turned to walk sadly back into the house.

The first thing we saw was Shandy sitting bolt upright on the front step head tilted in enquiry, watching the whole proceedings with interest. Stunned is not the word to describe how we felt. We looked from Shandy to the freshly turned soil and back again, before pouncing with cries of delight on our puzzled pet.

It turned out we had buried the farm cat from across the road. Shandy had spent most of the time he was missing with Rachael. She had been confined to bed with a minor illness and so, never one to pass up the chance of snuggling in a nice warm bed, Shandy had kept her company.

Down The Town

The district around Seaton Burn and Wideopen was expanding quite rapidly at that time, most of the new building being council housing.

A meeting of local councillors was held to decide on the type of surface to lay on a footpath between two of these estates. I am not sure whether these were local government or parish councillors, but I do know that reports of their deliberations was the source of much amusement. Apparently, they could not agree on which surface would be best and the argument had become quite heated. In a well meaning effort to pour oil on troubled water, one councillor had risen to his feet and suggested,

"Why don't we just put our heads together and lay wood blocks?"

My friend, Elizabeth and her family were to be beneficiaries of the new housing. I loved going to their cosy home, so was quite disappointed at the prospect of them moving. Elizabeth and her family lived in a two up, two down miner's cottage in the centre of one of two parallel rows facing each other across quite a broad street.

Down the centre of this space ran two rows of back to back toilets. They were of the flushing variety, with metal chains swinging from overhead cisterns, but in every other respect, were similar to the old netty in my grandparents back garden in upper Coquetdale.

That is to say, they had a six inch gap at the bottom of the doors so you could check whether or not they was occupied. Each door also had a row of three or four small circular holes drilled in them so as to be about eye level when you were "enthroned". This enabled occupants to spot anyone approaching and begin to sing or whistle to warn of their presence. I don't suppose the indoor toilet in Elizabeth's new house was half as much fun.

SOMEONE ELSE'S CAT.

"Has Shandy not come back yet?"
My little sister cried.
"Hush now" said mam,
"I'm sure he'll come
When it gets cold outside.

But through the chilly night time
Our hopes began to dim
And all day long
We felt so wrong
And still no sign of him.

How could a scrap of ginger
Leave such a yawning gap?
My mother sighed,
My sister cried,
But still he wasn't back.

What we all feared had happened,
My father brought him home,
No more to purr,
No golden fur,
The house was filled with gloom.

The garden was his graveyard,
We buried him with care.
With sorrowing sighs
We wiped our eyes
And turned———— and he was there!

Down The Town

Sitting on our doorstep
With patience, there he sat!
It dawned on us
We'd made a fuss
Of someone else's cat.

WIDEOPEN

As well as council housing, to Mam's delight, two new police houses were built in the neighbouring village of Wideopen and we were allocated one of them. This was luxury indeed. The houses had electricity! That meant electric lights instead of gas. No more fragile gas mantles giving off an eerie glow. Not only that, we had hot water flowing straight from the tap! Most amazing of all, we had a proper bathroom with a bath!

This was such a novelty that for months after we moved in, school friends of mine without such a "mod con" used to descend on us for a weekly bath. (Whether they needed it or not)

Mind you, despite all these mod cons, something basic seemed to have been forgotten - - - - insulation - - - - although there was a fireplace in the sitting room and a sort of poor relation to the Aga in the kitchen, the house was freezing in winter. I remember mam was so cold, she knitted herself some woolly kneepads!

One "friend" that I was glad to see the back of when we moved to Wideopen was a slightly older girl who had systematically but subtly bullied me from the day we arrived in Seaton Burn. There was no physical cruelty involved, it was purely mental torture. Nothing that you could explain to an adult, and nothing specific that I can remember now.

I just remember that the upshot of it was that I was completely under the thumb of this girl, who, in the guise of being my friend, controlled my every waking moment, and I accepted it as part of life. Wideopen was bliss without her. I did encounter her again at secondary school, but she had found other victims with which to amuse herself by then.

Looking back, I wonder how I could have allowed this complete subjugation of myself to happen.

I was a shy and introverted child at that time, but reasonably intelligent, with a good mother who would have helped me, had I made her aware of my plight. Yet I suffered for years and no one knew. Bullying often goes unnoticed. There do not necessarily need to be bruises, child perpetrators are adept at disguising mental cruelty and victims are often unbelievably stoic.

The two Wideopen houses had an office sandwiched between them, with access from both homes, so there was no longer any need for the police telephone to be in our living room.

This was a fact for which I was very thankful.

Many were the times that father's temper would explode when he was on the phone in our Seaton Burn sitting room.

Linda and I were well trained to cease all talking, even movement, when the huge black Bakelite police telephone rang, for it needed only the slightest sound, however accidental, for him to start yelling with rage. No doubt he was often tired. His beat covered Seaton Burn, Wideopen, and miles of surrounding countryside, all of it on foot or bicycle.

There were other policeman, the wonderful Frankie Douglas and his lovely wife, Marie at Dudley, Jock Thompson and his wife, (Margaret I think) at Hazlerigg, and Reggie and Molly Knight at Dinnington village. They all covered for each other on their days off, but, living in the midst of the community, as they did, they were effectively on duty twenty four hours a day, as were their wives.

Whatever the reason, we all became used to "walking on our eyelashes" whenever father was around. Poor mam often bore the brunt of his temper, and not being the type to fight back, became more and more subjected to bullying. The only time I saw her defy him was once when Linda had had the temerity to whisper something to me when he was on the phone.

He completely lost his temper and his terrifying bulk lunged at us, trying to wallop us. Fortunately, we had taken refuge under the table, so he was frustrated in this aim, which, of course, only served to make him even more furious. Seeing the danger we were in, mam quickly flew to the kitchen, returning with the sweeping brush.

"Stop that now," she shouted. Something in her tone must have penetrated through the red mist, because he paused in his attack long enough to look up and see her wielding the brush.

"If you hit those bairns, I'll set about you with this." Stated our gentle little mother with quiet determination. Amazingly, it worked, he calmed down and mam was able to hustle us out of harm's way.

Nerve wracking though he was to live with, father was a popular local "bobby". He ran a tight ship—— there was rarely any trouble on his beat, simply because trouble makers were summarily dealt with, so he was much admired by the law abiding section of the community. I remember a publican from "The Centurion" at Newburn once ringing the police station there in something of a panic because of a near riot which had broken out on his premises.

"Will you send three polisses, or Bob Nairn," he requested.

Down The Town

On one occasion at Seaton Burn, two drunks whose offensive behaviour was spoiling everyone's evening at a dance in the store hall, were grasped by their collars and the seat of their pants and hurled unceremoniously down the stairs, to the approval of everyone there!

Can you imagine the cries of "police brutality" not to mention the litigation that would have ensued nowadays?

He could be very kind too. One particularly cold winter, on discovering that an old lady had run out of coal to heat her house and was spending whole days in bed to keep warm, he took her a sack of coal from our coal house.

Mind you, mam was left with the problem of eking out our remaining coal as he didn't offer any extra housekeeping money to replace it, and there was no question of him having to suffer. As a result, the fire was allowed to go out when he was out on duty and we all froze until he came back.

He was a talented artist, pencil drawings and water colours were his specialities. He did this sketch of mam when she was 21

Dad's Pencil Sketch of Mam

There was no doubting his courage either. At nineteen he became the youngest sergeant in the British army and was decorated for valour.

One incident at Wideopen impressed me because it involved deep water. There was an old quarry next to the main road which had become flooded, forming an extremely deep steep sided pool.

Someone had drowned in it, so the body had to be retrieved. Father, being the local bobby was expected to do it.

 Even in uniform, father was rarely seen without a pipe clenched between his teeth, so, puffing on his pipe, he strode through the assembled crowd and scrambled down the bank.

He began to wade out towards the centre, feeling for the body in the murky water. Suddenly, he vanished from sight! He had stepped off a hidden shelf into much deeper water. There was a gasp from the crowd, then a cheer when he bobbed back up, complete with bobby's helmet and still puffing on his pipe! The quarry has since been filled in and there is a children's playground on the site.

As an effective upholder of law and order, (not Lauren Order, the mysterious person so beloved of T.V. and radio announcers) Father was expected to sit his sergeants exam to enable promotion to take place, however, this he stubbornly refused to do. As a result, one morning brought the exalted personage of the local police superintendent to our front door. Mam, Linda and I had never actually seen a real superintendent before, so we were quite overawed.

The poor man must have regretted his visit almost immediately because it was me who answered the door to find him standing next to a pint of milk on our front step. I picked up the milk and was about to invite him in, when my grip on the bottle slipped and the entire contents were somehow catapulted down the front of his uniform.

It was like throwing a bottle of milk over God! It must be said that he was a perfect gentleman about it, brushing off my and Mam's apologies as though he was attacked by milk throwing little girls every day of the week.

He succeeded in impressing mam and I, but had no luck with father, who still resolutely refused to sit the promotion exam. The reason being, he felt that some people had an unfair advantage by being sent on a detectives training course first.

The poor superintendent was sent off soaked with milk and with a flea in his ear about what father considered to be the injustices in the police promotion system.

THE POLISS'S PIPE.

"Quick, fetch the Polis,"
The people all cry.
"Tom's drowned in the quarry
Determined to die."

Sadly his family
Have searched night and day,
Though they knew when he vanished
He was gone to stay.

Now they all stare
At the dark quarry deep.
They wait for the poliss
And silently weep.

Here's big Bob now
Pipe clenched tightly, and grim
He strides through the crowd.
They look bleakly at him.

Down The Town

Straight into the water
He wades quickly out,
Pipe puffing with effort,
But then comes a shout!

He plummets quite suddenly
Right out of sight
The crowd holds it's breath
Hoping big Bob's all right.

Up pops a helmet,
Then their poliss appears
The sad faces suddenly
Grin ear to ear.

Up from the depths
Giving his face a wipe,
Still clenched in his teeth
And still smoking, his pipe!

JACKIE AND BLACKIE.

One of father's friends was a noted musician, Jack Armstrong. He lead a very popular country dance band called "The Barnstormers".

Not only that, he was the Duke of Northumberland's personal piper, so he cut an impressive figure when in his uniform of black and white Northumbrian "shepherd's plaid" with a set of the sweet sounding Northumbrian small pipes under his arm.

Jack Armstrong

Father first got to know him when Jack and his wife bought a plot of land near our police house at Wideopen.

They set about building their own bungalow, a task with which father was soon enthusiastically involved, whether they liked it or not! In fact, behind his back, the builder referred to father as "the gaffer".(No one ever called father anything to his face!)

The completed bungalow was most impressive, with its views of the distant Cheviots and popping in to visit the Armstrong's quickly became a favourite occupation with Linda and I. (The Cheviot view is now obscured by a housing estate.) We especially enjoyed visiting Mrs. Armstrong senior, who house sat the bungalow whenever Jack and his wife were away.

There were, in the sitting room, two beautiful bronze statuettes in the classical Greek style, which old Mrs. Armstrong allowed Linda and I to polish. At the time we were extremely proud of getting the statues to shine like new pennies.

It wasn't until years later, whilst watching "The Antiques Road show" that I found out that we had probably devalued them considerably by completely destroying their patina!

One of Jack's absences caused great excitement. He was off to Hollywood! The singer/actor, Burl Ives was a friend of his and so had invited Jack to Hollywood to record some Northumbrian pipe music for a film with which he was involved. Don't ask me what the film was, if I ever knew, I have quite forgotten now.

What I do remember clearly is that Jack met Marilyn Monroe! He watched her working on the film set and was captivated by her beauty, but also struck by how nervous she was.

"The poor lass is a nervous wreck, she breaks out in a rash every time it's her turn to act." He declared. Marilyn had charmed Jack completely. I often wonder what she thought of the gentle Northumbrian. He would certainly be very different from the type of men she usually met.

When he returned, Jack gave Linda and I a silver dollar each, which we still have.

Apart from his job as the local bobby, helping Jack with his building work, (and a fair amount of time spent socialising in the pubs on his patch) Father's remaining spare time was spent on creating a magnificent garden around our house. The pair of police houses had been built in the corner of a field (now Woodlands Park) and a good bit of field had been left as our garden.

It must have been a daunting task, but in no time, he had the land divided into four areas ——a neat little formal front garden, a rose garden, complete with rustic trellis at the side and at the back, an immaculate lawn surrounded by lush herbaceous borders. There was even room for a productive vegetable garden. The whole lot was surrounded by a beech and holly hedge.

The potato crop was so good that he decided to build a potato clamp in which to store some of the excess over the winter, so a pit was dug, lined with straw, filled with potatoes, then covered with layers of straw and earth. The finished article looked something like a mini central American pyramid, the ones with the flat tops built by the Aztecs.

We all forgot about it until later in the winter, father decided to open it up to retrieve some spuds for the larder. What followed was like a scene from a low budget horror movie

Down The Town

A tide of mice flowed from the disturbed clamp, completely engulfing Whisky, our old cat. He stood, knee deep in mice with a look of utter amazement on his face. By the time he regained his senses, they had run past him to where Linda and I stood, thunderstruck. We were so mesmerised by the scene that we hadn't the sense to get out of the way. Of course, the inevitable happened and a mouse ran up Linda's leg! It ran down again quite quickly, but that didn't matter. I think the screams would be heard at the other side of Newcastle! The mice dispersed and vanished, (goodness knows where to) and peace was restored.

It was while we lived at Wideopen that I came to understand the saying, "as mad as a March hare" for the first time. The fields behind our house where Woodlands park now stands, was full of wildlife, so in March, we were fascinated to see not one, but five hares apparently dancing about on their hind legs and boxing with each other in the field just outside our garden. They took no notice at all of our family peering at them over the fence and did appear to have taken leave of their senses. It was explained to me that this was part of a courting ritual. (Not unlike some behaviour I saw displayed in some rural dance halls in later years!)

When we moved to Wideopen, Shandy, our ginger cat had decided to stay with Rachel, but it wasn't long before we were back to our full complement of two. We still had old grey Whisky of course, and he was joined by a half grown semi long haired black cat with the rather prosaic name of "Blackie". We inherited him from the "Hadrian" shop around the corner. His job was to keep the mice down in the store room (perhaps that is where our potato clamp mice went)But the shop closed at weekends, so poor Blackie was slung out onto the street from Saturday lunch time until Tuesday morning, when the shop reopened.

Being a cat, it was not long before he found himself another billet, namely us. He was a lovely cat, but his early life as a rodent exterminator had left it's mark. He constantly eyed up the pet guinea pigs which lived in hutches in the little side yard. Linda and I had two each. Mine rejoiced in the names of Kenneth and Briege! I don't remember what names Linda's were blessed with, but no doubt they would be something equally unsuitable.

As we each had a boy and a girl guinea pig, nature took it's inevitable course and they produced babies. They were delightful little things, born complete with fur, like little pom poms, perfect miniatures of their parents. Mothers and babies had to be separated from the fathers though, as the dads were less than enchanted with their young, (Not unlike our own dear father!) so for a time they were kept in a box in the house.

This was just what Blackie had been waiting for ——bite sized guinea pigs! Despite our best efforts to prevent him, he defeated all our security measures and made off with one.

On discovering this tragedy, I ran to tell mam, who had a part time job in Connie Simpson's sweetie shop next door. I shrieked at her across the crowded shop,

"Mam, quick, the cat's had a guinea pig."

The puzzled look on her face should have told me to rephrase that, but I had turned on my heels and rushed back home in case Blackie should decide to make another raid.

We did manage to rear the rest safely and find good homes for them all.

No grudge was harboured against Blackie, after all, he was only doing what came naturally, in fact what his earlier livelihood had depended upon.

 The sweet shop owner, Connie Simpson's husband, Bob, worked at that time for the local paper, The Evening Chronicle. My mother must have been showing off to him my earliest efforts at writing rhymes, because the next thing I knew, much to my embarrassment at the time, A piece appeared about me in the "Eldon's Gossip" column. I think mam thought she had a child prodigy on her hands.

Just shows how wrong you can be. I was a grandmother before I put pen to paper again!

NORMA JEAN AND THE PIPER.

His pipes and plaid
Across the sea
Jack took to Hollywood.
The plaintive notes
He brought to them
Were sweetly played and good

The girl who played
A golden part
He found a fragile flower,
Entrapped within
The celluloid
The politics and power.

Down The Town

His northern heart
Reached out to her
With sympathy and care
But home called him,
And when she needed help
No one was there

THE HOPPINGS.

The position of the police house at Wideopen had several advantages, the main one being it's close proximity to the local cinema where I spent many a happy hour in the cheap seats at the front soaking up westerns, comedies and musicals with equal enjoyment. Mam rarely attended "the pictures", but I do remember her once accompanying Linda and I to a Danny Kay film which she particularly enjoyed.

One scene included the hapless Danny getting entangled in a ballet performance. Mam laughed so hard and so long that we began to attract the unwelcome attention of the other cinema patrons, but the more Linda and I tried to hush her, the more helplessly she laughed until each intake of breath became a screech like a rusty hinge. The only other person I've ever heard make a similar noise was Norman Wisdom in an old comedy duet 'Narcissus' with Joyce Grenfell, much played on the wireless in the fifties.

Mam's opportunities for leisure were few and far between. She did get involved with the local chapter of the "Women's Institute," where she made a lifelong friend, Eleanor (Nell) Winter. She also made occasional sorties on the bus down the town, or to her mother's at South Shields but other than that, her life was spent looking after home and family. (Keeping father's temper sweet was an uphill struggle, a thankless task condemned to frequent failure.)

She supplemented her meagre housekeeping by working part time in Mrs. Simpson's sweetie shop, conveniently situated just along the road, so spare time was scarce.

However, once a year she always managed to take us down the town to the "Hoppings", the annual travelling fair which still comes to Newcastle.

It is the world's largest travelling fair, attracting showmen from all over the country and then, as now, sprawled over about a hundred of the town moor's twelve hundred acres alongside the Great North Road.

The appearance of "The Hoppings" on the town moor was then, apart from Christmas, the highlight of every "Geordie" child's year.

Three long avenues of attractions belting out loud music made the heart beat faster and we clutched Mam's hand tightly as we passed the "Lost Children" tent on the way in.

The row nearest the road consisted of "roll the penny", "bingo," "hook the duck," shooting ranges, coconut shies and the like, all festooned with soft toys, plaster ornaments and unfortunate goldfish as prizes.

The bingo stalls had their regular customers who sought them out year after year and would not patronise any other stall.

The third row contained curiosities like the bearded lady, the flea circus, boxing rings where local lads queued up to be flattened, some stands with dancing girls, gyrating about the stage bedecked with tassels which defied all laws of motion, and all manner of attractions which claimed to be "educational"!

Best of all though was the middle row where the rides were set out. Helter skelters, big wheels, roundabouts with prancing horses or little cars and buses for the toddlers, Scarey rides where the screams of the punters drowned out the music, shuggy boats, dodgem cars, waltzers etc.

All of them were interspersed with food stalls selling hot dogs, toffee apples, coconuts, candy floss and all manner of confectionery. The smells combined with the music to lend an exotic and exciting air to the whole occasion, but the part I loved best was the area at the end nearest the town where the gypsy fortune tellers were gathered.

Here, mystery was in the air, as gypsy ladies of all ages tried to lure customers into the inner sanctums of their caravans, where, having crossed her palm with silver, the fortune tellers promised that the secrets of the future would be revealed. Some had traditional caravans, brightly painted and quaint, others favoured gleaming modern vans, but outside all of them boards were displayed covered in photographs of satisfied customers and famous clientele.

Our annual visit to "the Hoppings" was something to look forward to, even though, with spending money at a premium we were mainly spectators rather than participants. Mam always managed to let us have a go on "roll the penny", where we were each strictly dolled out three or sometimes four of the huge old fashioned pennies of the day. Once they were gone, Linda and I knew better than to ask for more, we knew very well the difficulty with which Mam had accrued this precious hoard.

Blissfully we wandered, transported for a while to a different world. Each year there was a turn on one of the many rides available. Choosing which one took far longer than the ride lasted, but that was all part of the fun.

One year, when I was about nine and Linda about six, Mam must have lowered her guard on the finances, because we spent the bus fare home and had to walk the six miles back from the town to Seaton Burn.

I know it was six miles because the pub along the road from our house was named "The Six Mile" in recognition of its exact distance from Newcastle.

Thankfully, that year was one when the sun shone on "the Hoppings" so, although our "shoes were full of feet" we at least arrived home weary but dry.

The week of the fair, even though in June, seemed to attract extremes in weather. It was always either red hot, reducing the Town Moor to a dust bowl, or, poured with rain, reducing it to a quagmire!

I would be about 14 when the weather reached such depths of awfulness that the Hoppings had to stay for another week so that the showmen could make up their losses, thus negating, for once, mam's favourite expression 'making money like a showman' meaning easily and in vast quantities.

SECONDARY SCHOOL.

Wideopen police house was also conveniently placed for the new Secondary modern school, which was to be my designated centre of education on reaching the age of eleven. All children then were required to sit the eleven plus exam, which sorted the sheep from the goats. It never even entered my head that there was any possibility of being anything other than one of the goats, and so it proved. The fact that some children from our class of over forty did pass the exam and go to Gosforth grammar (about half a dozen I think) speaks volumes for the dedication of our teacher, Mrs. Thompson.

The secondary school was a complete revelation to me. The teachers were young and exciting and we had different ones for each subject! I quickly discovered a love of English (language and literature) history, geography and art, whereas everything scientific left me completely mystified.

I am still of the school of thought that wonders why the electricity doesn't run out of the holes in the wall when I pull a plug out.

I turned out to be a pretty fair sprinter and long jumper, but useless at distance running, high jump, throwing things and all team games. Physical education at Seaton Burn Primary had consisted of "drill" standing in lines in the yard and the odd game of net ball, so the range of activities on offer here was exhilarating and the lessons inspiring.

The English teacher, Miss Willetts, introduced us to the magical world of Greek and Roman mythology. She was a tiny, fair, ethereal young woman with the most beautiful voice! Even now, when I'm reading, it is her voice I hear in my head.

By the time I started secondary school I had already been scribbling little verses in a note book for a couple of years, so I was fertile ground for an inspirational teacher like her.

It wasn't all beer and skittles though. At about the same time as all these new opportunities for learning became available, my eyesight suddenly deteriorated quite dramatically so that availing myself of them became difficult.

The last thing I wanted was to be forced to wear a pair of the ugly national health specs of the day, so I set about concealing the fact that I couldn't see.

A recent growth spurt had made me even taller for my age than I'd been before, so I was always put at the back of the class, where I was normally happy to blend into the background. Once my sight faded, being at the back of the class became a real problem though, because I couldn't see the board. In those days, a lot of lesson time was spent copying facts from the board, so I solved the problem by copying from my friend, Jean, who sat beside me.

I quickly learned to recognise approaching people by the sound of their footsteps and the way their general bulk moved, as general bulk was all I could see until they were right next to me. It was a bit of a strain, but I managed quite well, although the day the school medical examiner tested all our eyesight presented something of a challenge! When our teacher announced that the whole class was to report to the medical room for eye tests, my heart sank. The game would be up now and I could see a pair of pink wire rimmed specs beckoning. However, my luck was in, because the whole class was ushered into the capacious medical room all at once.

It was a simple matter to get to the end of the queue, sidle near to the eye chart and memorise it! I couldn't memorise it all of course, but I must have managed enough to fool the examiner. Owlish wire rimmed specs retreated into the distance once more.

This reprieve was to prove temporary. Some weeks later, I was busily copying from Jean's book whilst ostentatiously staring at the blur of chalk on the board, when into the classroom strode our head teacher, Mr. Mitchell. This was a rare event which set off alarm bells straight away. He wandered up and down the rows of desks, at random, nodding and smiling at good work, occasionally frowning and pointing at work not quite up to scratch. I soon realised with sinking heart that the apparent random nature of his wandering was, in fact, no such thing. He was unmistakably making for me! I kept my eyes glued to the page as I slowly transcribed the last few words I could remember from Jean's book.

His dark suited figure stood over me, watching as I squinted in vain at the board, then hunched, defeated in my seat.

"What's the matter Lorna? Can you not see the board?"

I tried one last desperate gambit.

"No sir, it's not that. The sun is shining on it so I just can't see from here."

Mr. Mitchell slowly lowered himself until his head was on a level with mine

"I can see it quite clearly from here Lorna." He said gently, and I knew in that moment that the game was up.

The optician down the town explained in simplified terms that my sudden spurt of growth had caused the problem — my eye muscles could not keep pace, rendering me extremely short sighted. The specs I was given weren't too bad, certainly not the pink wire framed horrors I had so dreaded, and the world leaped dramatically back into focus. So dramatically in fact that, walking out of the optician's door, I immediately took a nose dive into the street!

I do not know which of my teachers drew Mr. Mitchell's attention to my short sightedness, but, as a result he continued to take an interest in my progress, encouraging my efforts at writing poetry, and, eventually, putting me up as a candidate for the thirteen plus exam.

The only other unhappy memory I have of Wideopen Secondary Modern involved a domestic science class on open day and two greedy girls.

The school was buzzing, open day was coming up, and as a new school, it was important that a good impression was made. Classrooms were set out with examples of good work, science labs and wood and metal workshops were laid out to impress, but it was the domestic science room which concerned me.

It was not a subject at which I excelled, but my class drew the short straw and ours was to be the honour of showing off the results of our culinary expertise. Each girl was told what to cook for the display, and of course, in those days, we provided our own ingredients. I was to make a fresh fruit salad. The teacher, knowing my ability to produce disasters from every type of oven in the room, was probably playing safe, but ours was a house where fresh fruit was a luxury, so it was with some diffidence that I asked Mam if she could provide the ingredients.

I needn't have worried, she did me proud and the fruit salad, when completed on the morning of open day, was a work of art.

It included apples, oranges, bananas, even such exotic items as peaches and grapes! I was tremendously proud of my effort, and basking in my teacher's approval, couldn't wait for the afternoon when Mam and all the other parents would view my masterpiece.

It was to be the first time in my life that I realised the truth in the saying, "Pride comes before a fall." Towards the end of the lunch break I strolled happily into the domestic science room, just to check that the fruit salad didn't need a final tweak.

I was appalled by the sight that met my eyes.

Floating about in a bowl of liquid were a few slices of apple, a couple of pieces of soggy banana and a solitary green grape.

Two plump girls, no, I won't beat about the bush, two FAT girls, from the year above stood smirking in the corner of the room and began to giggle when they saw the horrified look on my face.

They put their hands over their mouths to cover their sniggers, but not before I had seen the unmistakable glisten of the sticky fruit juice which covered their mouths and chins.

Anger was replaced by fury, when the two gluttonous thieves denied their crime, and in the absence of concrete proof, got away with it.

The Decimated Fruit Salad

It was Mam's reaction I was worried about. I knew how hard those ingredients had been for her to provide, and for them to vanish down the throats of two greedy lumps before she had even seen them was almost more than I could bear. I don't know how Mam felt, but I found the incident unutterably depressing. I still find gluttony one of the least attractive of the seven deadly sins. If I had known in advance about the two thieves, I would have laced the fruit salad with syrup of figs!

Secondary school broadened my horizons in more ways than one. As well as varied and interesting lessons, there were varied and interesting people too.

We had a visit from two charming young teachers from Trinidad and Tobago (one from each island) who opened our minds to the rich variety of the earth and its people.

On a much smaller scale, I met, for the first time, children from nearby villages who all attended Wideopen Secondary Modern. My closest friends at Seaton Burn school had included Jean Mordue, Eileen Hancock (otherwise known as "Iggle") Valerie Calvert, who had a beautiful singing voice, Elizabeth Hunter, Valerie Hay, Valerie Turnbull, (popular name then, Valerie) Bruce Tinsley and his sister Freda, Ken Gibson, and various others.

Into my circle of acquaintances came people like Marlene Patinson from Dinnington, Lydia Stephenson and Anna Wise from Hazlerigg and Doreen Maloney from Brunswick village.

Doreen was a remarkably pretty girl who would have made an excellent Snow White, with her huge greenish hazel eyes, lustrous dark hair, delicate skin and a way of wrapping even the most hardened teachers round her little finger. A real charmer was Doreen.

The only school trips I remember going on in my life were, I think, all from Wideopen school. One, to Housesteads on the Roman wall served to confirm my fascination with history. The other two were to York and Edinburgh, places I would never have had the opportunity to visit otherwise, so I am eternally grateful to whoever it was who organised those expeditions.

Down The Town

Very few children had access to private cars then, so school trips were an extremely valuable experience.

There were two things which interfered with my complete happiness at Wideopen, both of them inflicted on me by mam, thinking they would be good for me. One was the local chapter of the Brownies and the other was piano lessons.

The Brownies met in a dilapidated hut between Wideopen and Hazlerigg road end and I think mam got the idea from Mrs Thompson, the policeman's wife from Hazlerigg. Her two daughters, Margaret and Kathleen, were both enthusiastic Brownies so I was despatched to join the troop. I hated it from the word go. First of all, I couldn't get my head around having to call grown women "Brown Owl" and "Tawny Owl". It was ridiculous! They patently were not owls, they were middle aged ladies in sensible shoes.

I hated the little tasks they set us for which we earned badges which then had to be neatly and laboriously sewn onto our sleeves, thus making it immediately apparent who were the top dogs and who were falling down on the job.

The final straw was when we were tested on our ability to darn a hole in a sock. With clenched teeth, I laboured long at this boring task.

The finished piece of work, though I say it myself, was a very creditable effort and I bore it with pride to the Brownie hut. However, waiting outside for "Brown Owl" to come and open up, I was invited to compare my repaired sock with that of another girl. Like an idiot, I fell for it and before I knew it, the two pieces of darning had been swapped and, needless to say, I came off worst in the deal!

The other girl was a long established member of the troop and a great favourite of the pair of owls in charge, so it seemed futile to complain. I seethed inwardly as she was praised and given top marks for my piece of work, while my substituted offering was grudgingly passed as "adequate".

That was it. Never a child to rebel, I nevertheless put my foot down and refused to go back to the Brownies. It was the beginning of a long career of managing to avoid joining group activities of any kind. I am most definitely not a "joiner".

I wasn't much good at the other activity mam selected for me either. Goodness knows where it came from, but, when we moved into the new house at Wideopen, a very ornate upright piano was established in pride of place in the sitting room. It even had brass candlesticks which swivelled out at either side of the music stand. Liberace would not have been ashamed of it.

To justify its existence I was sent for piano lessons. First of all to a kindly man at Hazlerigg road end. I was a dreadful pupil, not prepared to put in the practice needed when I could have been hurtling up and down Brunswick lane on my roller skates. I much preferred to "wing it" and play tunes by ear. Eventually, my teacher, more in sorrow than in anger, informed mam that she was wasting her money. To sweeten the pill, he sent me away with an enormous Cox's Orange Pippin apple from the tree in his back garden. Delicious!

Poor mam must have been desperate to have someone in the family who could play the piano, because, in spite of the cost, which she could ill afford, she had another crack at turning me into Winifred Atwell. I was despatched to another teacher just along the road.

A woman this time, she was not prepared to stand for any nonsense, so I struggled along for a while and managed to pick up the basics, but that was as far as it went. When mam discovered me, for the umpteenth time, reading my "School Friend " girl's comic tucked inside the music I was supposed to be practising, she gave in.

By this time the list of things I had failed at was pretty long so no one had any high expectations when I was dispatched off to Morpeth, along with several of my class mates, to sit the thirteen plus exam. I did my best and then forgot about it.

CELEBRATIONS.

There were two notable celebrations in our house at Wideopen, both of them were family weddings.

I don't remember which one came first, as there wasn't much time between them, but both dad's hill shepherd brothers from the Coquet valley, uncles Bill and Jim were married and had their receptions at our house. Both married beautiful young women, although entirely different from each other.

Uncle Bill's bride was Bett Brodie, the elder of the two lovely Brodie girls from Blind burn in Upper Coquetdale. (See "Up the Valley") She was as lovely as a ripe peach, with dark blonde hair, a beautiful complexion and an entertaining turn of phrase. Linda and I were considered too young to attend the party (although there are actually not many years between Bett and myself) so we sat on the stairs and watched the proceedings from there.

The house was heaving with people, many of them from Coquetdale, including Bett's younger brother Dode, whom Linda and I thought delicious and secretly lusted after for years! He was a good looking young chap, who, when home from the sea, was prone to hurtle up and down the Coquet valley at alarming speeds on his motor bike. It got to the pitch when the people up the valley timed any journeys they had to make so as to avoid meeting Dode either on his way out of the valley or on his way back home!

Jack Armstrong was there, playing first the pipes (Northumbrian of course) then the accordion. Someone bashed a tune out of our old piano, drinks began to flow and all together the atmosphere was most convivial, to say the least!

That night when all their wedding guests had gone, Bett and Bill and Mary and Jim set off for Newcastle to round off their day "down the town".

Unfortunately, they got on the wrong bus coming back and got comprehensively lost. Eventually, they ended up at Dinnington and had to walk the rest of the way back to our house, where the bridal couple collapsed, exhausted onto the marriage bed in our spare room.

Unfortunately, someone, (and Dode's name was mentioned, but father's, was too so who the real culprit was I don't know) had "doctored" the double bed. They hadn't been upstairs very long when there was the most almighty clatter. The bed completely disintegrated, dumping the happy but weary couple unceremoniously on the floor!

Uncle Jim's wedding celebration followed a similar pattern. His bride was a tiny vivacious dark haired Scottish lass called Mary. She was the daughter of the Denham family who had moved into Windyhaugh farm in upper Coquetdale after my grandparents vacated it. She looked exactly like a dark haired version of the film star, Glynis Johns, and with my tall fair haired uncle Jim, they made a fine looking couple.

Aunty Mary

Unfortunately there are no photographs of Mary in existence before the age of about forty, but she is still an extremely pretty woman today.

I don't remember any tricks being played on them, but I could be wrong. I can't think that they'd escape unscathed. Maybe I just never found out about it.

I do remember aunty Mary coming to my rescue when I had a nasty infection where a splinter had entered my hand. The whole thing had turned septic and needed to be lanced. Mam was not looking forward to the trip to the doctor, so aunty Mary, never one to duck any job, offered to take me. This was probably a smart move, because, whereas I might have caused a fuss with mam, I submitted to the whole ordeal quietly with Mary in charge. Well I couldn't show myself up in front of my new aunty, could I?

The other celebration which I remember from Wideopen was one new years eve. Mam and dad had been invited to see the new year in at the home of Reggie and Molly Knight, the policeman at Dinnington and his wife. Linda and I were too young of course, so we were baby sat by a kind young woman called Hazel, a great favourite of ours as she made clothes for our dolls and occasionally took us on bus trips to Plessey Woods. Thus assured of our safety, mam set off for her first real new year party.

She set off quietly enough, but we all heard her coming back! The giggling , bumps and shrieks from downstairs woke everyone up in the early hours of the morning. Hazel bravely went to the top of the stairs and called down,

"Are you all right Mrs Nairn?"

"Helloooo Hazel, helloooo girls, I've had a lo-o-ovely time." Answered mam in the sort of girlish giggly voice I did not associate with her at all.

She set off up the stairs bouncing off the wall and the banister all the way up, like something in a pin ball machine! Father followed behind grinning from ear to ear and holding out his arms to prevent her falling backwards down the stairs. Hazel ushered Linda and I back into our bedroom and closed the door. She tucked us back into bed with a smile and settled down on her "shaky down" on the floor.

Eventually, silence prevailed and the house slept.

Next morning, mam was late rising and looked decidedly green about the gills. Sitting at the kitchen table with her head in her hands, she puzzled over what might be wrong with her.

"I only had a couple of snowballs and then I drank lemonade after that, " she moaned.

"Aye, but you didn't see what Reggie was putting in your lemonade," laughed father.

This one experience of a hangover was enough to frighten mam off drinking. For the rest of her life. She was always very careful not to "exceed the dose." In fact, the only other time she ever got "tiddly" was when, in her late sixties, Linda and I took her on holiday to Tenerife and she thought sangria was fruit juice! Rising to her feet at the end of a lovely meal in a pleasant restaurant, she declared in alarm.

"There's something the matter with me, my feet won't work!"

Linda took her firmly by the arm and explained,

"You've heard the expression, legless mother? Well that's what you are."

It took the two of us, one at each arm, to steer her safely back to our apartment.

HOLIDAYS

Linda and I were fortunate in that we had nana and granda and aunts and uncles living in the Northumbrian countryside, where we could spend carefree summers out of father's way, running wild. Mam and dad however, never went away on holiday, and , apart from the odd overnight stay when collecting us from relatives, never spent nights away from home.

Father did, on a couple of occasions, borrow Jackie Armstrong's car, and, on his days off, shuttle his family around Northumberland showing us the many farms on which his childhood had been spent.

His childhood had been spent in some of the most isolated and beautiful parts of Northumberland including one place along the Tarset Burn where Nana kept her hens in an old 'Bastle House' which is now the pride of English Heritage.

I absolutely adored these outings. Father had a deep love of his home county which he passed on effortlessly to us. I was in heaven being driven around the most beautiful and fascinating county in England. It amazes and disappoints me that children today are more likely to fall asleep or play with an electronic game than look out of the window on a journey. I suppose travelling by car is commonplace for them, whereas it was an exceptional treat for me.

The first time we went on a holiday as a family, I was about twelve years old, so Linda must have been eight or nine. Granda had acquired a little black car, like a camera on wheels, so we set off on the bus to their home. At this time they were living at Temperly Grange, a farm between Corbridge and Slaley and granda was becoming a well known danger on the roads in the vicinity.

To my knowledge, granda sat his driving test at least ten times. I'm not at all sure that he ever passed it! I remember one journey when he was driving nana and I to visit some distant relative who lived along a narrow winding road with a bit of a drop down one side. Nana became very agitated.

"Stop this car now Jack Nairn and let me and the bairn out." She yelled. Granda took no notice at all except to smile and say with a derisory snort,

"Hadaway woman!" whilst continuing to steer the car precariously close to the edge of the road. Nana in extreme terror, played her trump card.

"I'll tell our Bob where you're tekin' his dowter."

His only reaction to this was to speed up, making nana squeal like a stuck pig, and granda laugh uproariously. I enjoyed the whole escapade.

The Car Journey

Anyway, the plan was for father to borrow the car and with some basic camping equipment aboard, we were going touring up the west coast of Scotland.

It was wonderful! We headed west along the Roman wall— which I knew all about after my school trip to Housesteads of course. Then we took off through beautiful Dumfries and Galloway. Somewhere there we camped for the night in a field full of cows. I can't for the life of me imagine why dad selected that particular site, unless he was nostalgic for our tilted house in Davison St., Newburn, because, as well as being an object of fascination to every cow in the field, our tent was on a definite slope. We knew better than to mention this to father though if we wanted to survive the holiday, so we set about making ourselves comfortable for the night. It wasn't too bad, apart from the occasional cow crashing about outside, so we got to sleep quite quickly.

Morning was announced by mam shouting in alarm,
"Bob, where's the bairn?"
I sat up, staring at the empty space beside me where Linda had been the night before.

"I'm buggered if I know," muttered father, scrambling out of the tent on his hands and knees. Mam and I crawled out after him, to find him grinning and pointing. A little way down the slope, in the centre of a circle of curious cows, all chewing the cud with solemn deliberation, lay Linda, curled up and fast asleep. She had rolled out under the side of the tent during the night. I thought she did very well to avoid rolling in any cow pats considering the number of them about.

After a bacon and egg breakfast fried over a tiny primus stove, we set off again.

On through the pretty county of Kirkcudbright with it's white painted farms set in emerald green fields. We learned how to pronounce it correctly too — "Kirkoobry," which I thought was much nicer than it's spelling.

And so, on into Ayrshire, where, just south of the seaside town of Girvan, whilst struggling up a steep hill, Granda's car gave up the ghost.

I didn't know then what the "big end" in a car was, but whatever it was, it went, rendering the little car completely useless. We all piled out, unloaded our gear and set up camp by a stream at the bottom of the hill. And that was where we stayed for the rest of our holiday, until the garage in Girvan got the car back on it's feet, so to speak. Linda and I were quite happy playing by the stream, but father's temper was tested up to and beyond it's limit by our mishap. I don't think it was a happy time for mam.

When the repaired car was left at nana and granda's at Temperly Grange, near Corbridge so was I. My cousin Alan was living with them at this time, so we resumed our long tradition of looking for mischief about the farm. Apart from getting lost in the wood behind the house, and driving nana mad with anxiety by vanishing for most of one day when we walked to Slaley and back, we spent a relatively blameless two weeks.

It was at that time I discovered you can't always believe what you read in adverts. One of nana's magazines claimed that if the face was massaged with lather from a particular soap, then wrinkles would disappear and the said face would have beauty to rival Helen of Troy. Determined to restore my much loved nana to the state of beauty which had been hers as a young woman, I persuaded her to pause in her labours, and lie back on the settee. With due care, I worked up a creamy lather and gently massaged her face. After about half an hour, nana was asleep. Waking her up, I carefully wiped away the soap and declared with cruel honesty,

" Well it hasn't worked nana, you still look old!"
With a wry smile nana replied,
    "The trouble is I still feel it an' all."

It was on this visit to Temperley Grange that I caused my grandparents no end of amusement by suggesting that the stone built farm buildings would make beautiful houses. They laughed uproariously at the idea. I wish they were alive today to see the luxury "farm conversions" that exist there now!

Nana Nairn as a young woman.

MUSIC MUSIC MUSIC

My taste in music gradually moved on from Harpo Marx.

Popular singers of the day included Bing Crosby, Teresa Brewer, Lita Rosa, Guy Mitchell, Dickie Valentine (I wonder who gave him that name!) David Whitfield, Rosemary Clooney, (aunt of the gorgeous George.) Joan Regan, Ruby Murray, (forever immortalised in cockney rhyming slang for curry) Frankie Laine, Doris Day, Alma Cogan etc.

They sang songs with titles like "Never do a tango with an Eskimo", "The railroad runs through the middle of the house" and "Where will the baby's dimple be" and what is more, we were prepared to listen to them! It was a tremendous leap from them to the new generation of singers and musicians, but one which I took my time in making.

Rock n roll arrived just as I entered my teens. I was no pushover for its charms though. My friend, Jean, was besotted by Britain's answer to the American rockers, Tommy Steele, and, while I had to admit that he was lively, his appeal completely passed me by. I had listened to Elvis Presley on the wireless and cared nothing for him either.

All this changed one evening in the cheap seats of the local cinema with an item on the news reel which always preceded the main feature. A black and white film showed the young Elvis singing "All Shook Up" from what appeared to be an open air boxing ring. That was it! I was hooked!

In those days there were no such thing as teenagers. Everyone dressed either as a child or as a cut down version of their parents. I was the former at this stage, but the early signs of "teendom" were there.

The walls of the bedroom which I shared with Linda began to display pictures of my new heart throbs and I began to save up my meagre pocket money to buy the recordings of the singers I admired. These, of course, were the old seventy eights, huge and fragile. It took me weeks to save up for one, so they were very precious. The day father sat on one of them was a major tragedy, but one which had to be born in silence for fear of rousing his temper.

The posters on my bedroom wall once gave mam's friend, Nell a rude awakening. We had moved away from Wideopen, so Nell and husband Harrison were visiting for a couple of days. I vacated my double bed and moved in with Linda for the duration of their stay, but the entire household was wakened early by a piercing scream from Nell. She had opened her eyes to be confronted by a double page sized portrait of Sammy Davis Jnr. fixing her with his good eye from the bedroom wall!

Apart from Elvis, others on whom my teenage devotion was bestowed over the next few years included Paul Anka, Connie Francis, Rickie Nelson, Gene Vincent, Eddie Cochran, Bobby Darin and Brenda Lee and from the British contingent, Marty Wilde, (father of Kim) Billy Fury and Cliff Richard.

There were no radio programmes to cater specifically for emerging new types of music and T.V. was still a rarity so it was a case of listening to programmes such as "Two way family favourites" on Sunday lunch times hoping to hear a nugget of gold among what I, with the arrogance of youth, considered to be musical dross.

Later, when we did eventually acquire a T.V., my favourites were shows like "Juke Box Jury" with Pete Murray, David Jacobs and, representing the views of the general public, a girl called Janice with an atrocious Birmingham accent, whose sole attraction was the way she delivered her verdict, "Oi'll give it foive."

The Perry Como Show," imported from America, was a great favourite too. Not that I was a particular fan of Perry himself, but his show always featured an appearance by a teen idol of the day. I particularly remember my first sighting of the Everly brothers on his show, even mam was smitten by them! Father remained rabidly anti Perry Como, Mainly because he was American I think. Then, as now, that was reason enough for some people!

Later, I was an avid follower of the I.T.V. rival to Juke Box Jury, "Oh Boy." This was much more exciting because it featured live performances. Regulars on the programme included "The John Barry Seven," (Later of James Bond film music fame) Cherry Wainer, the diminutive organist, whose tiny stiletto heeled feet flew over the organ peddles; Joe Brown, the floppy haired singer/ guitarist (father of singer, Sam Brown) Marty Wilde, Cliff Richard etc. The producer, Jack Good, also wrote a column in the New Musical Express.

He must have been a nice man, because he took the time to answer at length my puerile teenage fan letter. I heard many years later that he had retired to a monastery which seems extreme lengths to go to to avoid fan mail. I hope he found happiness there.

We didn't watch only music shows, T.V. opened up the whole world to us.

We loved wildlife programmes and those which showed us how the people of other countries lived. On one occasion, mam, Linda and I spent a week eagerly anticipating a programme which, the announcer promised, would be very interesting, "The Leg Growers of Brazil."

Down The Town

We spent the week wondering how they managed to grow legs.

Were they perhaps a sort of mutation with three legs, hidden away in the rain forests? Or, and here my imagination ran riot, perhaps they grew legs as a crop. I envisaged fields of waving legs and wondered how they harvested them.

At last the day arrived and the three of us made ourselves comfortable in front of the television set. Excitement mounted as the preceding programme drew to a close and the announcer intoned,

"And now for the leg growers of Brazil."
We were much chastened to see the title come up on the screen,
"The leg rowers of Brazil!"

There followed an interesting documentary about a tribe of people who used their legs to row their boats! After we'd stopped laughing, we settled down and enjoyed the programme.

<u>NEWBURN AGAIN!.</u>

In those days, Policemen had no choice but to live in police accommodation. This was so that they could be moved about the county more or less at the whim of their superiors. Considerations such as children's education or any other inconvenience to the policeman's family did not figure at all.

Police houses varied considerably in size and quality, so it was the luck of the draw what you ended up with. Whatever you did end up with, every nut, bolt and light bulb had to be there when you left. A STRICT inventory was made on your arrival, and woe betide you if there was so much as a curtain runner missing when you moved out as the inventory was physically checked by a police inspector no less!

It didn't pay to get too attached to your home either, The "powers that be" didn't believe in leaving any policeman too long in one place in case he got too familiar with the locals and inclined to be too lenient, or, worse, open to bribery! Anyone who had the temerity to object to where they were posted was sent to a "Punishment station".

These were never officially acknowledged as such, but everyone knew, that if you were sent, for example, to Blanchland, with it's huge cold damp rat infested house in a village frequently cut off in the winter, it was because you had refused a move to somewhere else. Nowadays, of course, I am sure people would queue up to go to beautiful Blanchland with its more modern police house and today's better communications.

The other reason for moving policemen about the county was promotion. Father had finally been prevailed upon to sit his sergeant's exam, and passed it. (I believe that he agreed to the exam only on the promise of a place on the detective training course.) Because of his success, we had to be moved away from Wideopen, which was not a sergeant's station. The word came that we were to return to Newburn.

This time it was not to the house in Davison St. but to the actual Police station itself. This was an imposing, rather grim looking building on the main road between Newburn and Throckly.

Newburn Police Station, Now closed and up for sale.
My bedroom was the double window second from the left

The station was flanked by two houses on one side and one on the other. We were allocated the end one of the pair. Our next door neighbours were P.C. Jimmy Neesham, his wife and daughter, Kathleen.

The single house on the other side of the station was occupied by Sergeant Jardine, his wife and their son, Ian.

It was a complete change from our modern house at Wideopen, a sturdy old building, but at least it was warm, and mam could dispense with her woolly knee caps. There was a large communal police yard at the back of the building and at the opposite side of the yard to the houses were three long gardens. It must have been galling for father to leave the beautiful garden he had created at Wideopen, but I never heard him complain, and he was soon busy planting flowers and vegetables in his new strip of land.

Last time I saw Newburn Police Station, it was a sad sight, with its windows all boarded up, but it was a hive of activity in those days. Policemen from the surrounding area all worked from it, so there was always something going on and laughter was often heard echoing around the yard. Some of the policemen had an irreverent sense of humour and a taste for practical jokes.

The Inspector, whilst not permanently based there, was a regular visitor. He had a little office just off the main police office into which he would vanish, stoke up his pipe, and settle down to catch up with his paper work.

On one of his visits, his pipe must have been left lying around where some young constable had access to it, because someone (I'm not saying who) packed the bowl of the pipe with live match heads, so that when he lit it, it shot up like a rocket, singing the inspector's eyebrows and making a burn mark on the ceiling.

The Exploding Pipe

He must have been a very longsuffering man, because that wasn't the last time his pipe was tampered with. Next time he got his own back on them though. On this occasion, someone had packed his pipe with rubber shavings. The conspiratorial smiles when the inspector vanished into his office for a smoke soon vanished, when he re-emerged, puffing thick clouds of black foul smelling smoke, and there he stayed, in the general office, smoking his pipe to the bitter end until all of them were coughing and had tears streaming from their eyes! His pipe was never interfered with again.

Down The Town

One day when there wasn't much doing, a young P.C. decided to make himself useful by clearing out a large store cupboard in the police yard. He discovered all manner of police notices inside, which he then proceeded to festoon about the yard. The door of the outside toilet bore a sign saying "BEWARE OF FLOODING" and other signs were placed to hilarious effect on cars, buildings and bicycles. A good laugh was had by all before he was made to tidy them away again.

When we moved back to Newburn, I had sat the thirteen plus examination, but hadn't yet had the result. Until this came through, I attended the Wallbottle campus school. This was a set up which in theory sounds a very good idea. There were two schools on the site then, a secondary modern and a grammar school.

As I understand it, children could move freely between the schools, depending on their expertise in each subject. However, I wasn't there long enough to test the theory, because news came that I had, to my amazement, passed the thirteen plus exam!

One would have assumed that I would simply transfer to the grammar school on the campus or even go to the nearby grammar school at Lemington. Not a bit of it! I had been entered for the exam from Wideopen and everyone who passed the exam from there was allocated a place at the brand new grammar school at Westmoor.

The fact that I now lived right across the other side of town from Westmoor was not taken into account. As a result I spent a goodly part of the next eighteen months on the number sixty two bus!

WESTMOOR GRAMMAR SCHOOL.

It was on the said bus that I read the momentous news over someone's shoulder that a plane crash had taken the life of Buddy Holly. The rest of the journey was spent in a sort of numb shock, and the whole school was very subdued that day.

The journey from home to school began at seven twenty in the morning. The first leg took me to the north end of Scotswood bridge, the terminus for the 62 bus. I didn't get off until the other terminus at Westmoor, so, once installed in my seat, I could relax and gaze out of the window as I was soon "gannin alang the Scotswood road".

The bus quickly filled up with workers heading for their shift at Vickers Armstrong engineering works, which seemed to fill up most of the south side of the road, blocking any view of the river Tyne beyond. In fact, the whole of Scotswood road had the aspect of a L.S. Lowery painting, with its industry along one side and row upon row of two up two down terraced houses, liberally punctuated by pubs on the other.

I heard years later that the son of a friend, whilst working as an apprentice at the Vickers Armstrong engineering works had a very uncomfortable journey home one evening. He had made a 'bleezer' for his mother. In those pre central heating days the metal sheet used to put in front of the fire to blaze it up was a vital piece of equipment and every home had one. If a couple weren't speaking they were 'chalking on the 'bleezer''.

Anyhow this chap made his mam's 'bleezer' out of rolled steel and being already encumbered by a haversack, in order to carry it home, and to keep it from the prying eyes of the security man he had stuffed it under his jumper and down the front of his trousers.

A double decker hove into view and with some difficulty our hero climbed on board. It wasn't so much the weight of the metal that was causing the problem but the fairly sharp lower edge of the 'bleezer' which each time he took a step up threatened to cut off his 'family jewels'. The bus conductor (remember those?) blocked his access to the lower deck

"No room in here mate, you'll have to go upstairs".

The journey to the upper deck was excruciating and once there he discovered that it was impossible to sit down. Heart sinking, he heard the bus conductor approaching

"You can't stand up here son, sit yourself down".

Rather than try to explain why he couldn't sit down, our young friend opted to go back down stairs, another dangerous and painful exercise, which he achieved by hopping down each step. He was able to ride the rest of the way home on the platform as the conductor remained upstairs collecting fares. The 'bleezer' however wasn't done with him yet, as on the jump down from the bus, it almost delivered the 'coup de grace'. I hope his mother was grateful for the gift which almost turned her son into her daughter!

After Scotswood Road the next leg of the journey took me right through the centre of Newcastle. The passengers changed to office and shop workers and the cityscape we passed was extremely grand in places, relics of "the town's" wealthy past.

As the bus progressed through the town, I became a little anxious as the part of the journey I dreaded approached. This was the drive across Byker bridge. To me, this tall spindly looking structure did not look strong enough to carry any traffic, let alone a fully laden double decker bus. No white knuckle ride I've encountered since has given me whiter knuckles than the brief trundle across Byker bridge.

With relief I watched Shields road pass by, then the turn at the top before Chillingham road. The bus depot was near here, so sometimes there was a wait, while we swapped drivers, then off again along Chillingham road.

The next landmark was the accurately named Four Lane Ends and by now there was a sprinkling of the distinctive grey and maroon of our school uniform aboard the bus. As we passed between the two halves of the Longbenton estate, more and more grey and maroon clad figures boarded the bus and a mile later, when we reached the terminus, outside the school, a flood of pupils were disgorged to pour into the schoolyard.

The time by now was usually 8:35. I could have got a later bus, but the 62 only ran every twenty minutes then, so the next bus, although supposed to arrive at Westmoor at 8:55, was too chancy for me to risk— rush hour traffic often made it late and that would never do. The same journey in reverse took me home at night, then there was usually two hours of homework before I could call my time my own.

The distinctive grey and maroon uniform gave mam something of a headache. It included an overcoat and hat, as well as a blazer, pinafore dress and all the gear necessary for games and P.E., or P.T. as it was then called.

The whole thing was very expensive, unfortunately, father was one of those men who regarded his salary as his own personal pocket money.

There wasn't that much of it in the first place, policemen being some of the lowest paid members of society in those days, and the small amount he passed on to mam only just covered the family's day to day needs because my mother was something of a miracle worker in that department. This was one miracle, however, which was beyond her capabilities. Even her current job as a Phonataz girl (cleaning telephones for businesses) earned nowhere near enough to provide me with the required uniform.

I, of course was oblivious to the worry this gave my mother, and father took the view that it was nothing to do with him. However, when the day came, I was kitted out in full uniform and never gave it a thought. Years later, I discovered that one of mam's wonderful sisters had come to the rescue and loaned her the money needed.

I was delighted to find that Westmoor Grammar reunited me with some familiar faces from Wideopen school. Lydia Stephenson, Anna Wise and the dazzling Doreen Maloney were all there.

Westmoor Grammar School Circa 1958

Back Row
James Bamborough   Colin Oliver   William Davison   Robert Donachie   Godfrey Fenwick   Jeffrey Bailey   Alexander Brown   James Stephenson   John Hale   Ian McGregor

Middle Row
Gordon Beck   Brian Magillan   **Lorna Nairn**   Marion Davison   Doreen Armstrong   Linda Jackson   Nancy Grubb   Katherine Lothian   Russell Clark   Alan Wheatley

Front Row
Valerie Bushby   Hazel Thompson   Lydia Stephenson   Agnes Levison   Mr. J. Poll   Doreen Maloney   Anna Wise   Joyce McKenzie   Dorothy Brown   Hillary White

132

It was reassuring to see them, but it was a girl I'd never met before who was to become my lifelong friend, even though for most of our lives we have lived at opposite sides of the world.

Her name was Marion Davison and, like me, she had a long bus journey to school each day, as she lived on a farm in Prestwick Village, Ponteland. (Near Newcastle Airport.) Marion was a quiet girl and like me, tall for her age. She had a serenely pretty face with light turquoise blue eyes and curly blonde hair. We were thrown together because we were both tall, so our form teacher, when allocating seats, put us together at the back of the class. It proved to be an inspired decision on his part, we were friends from then on.

Marion aged 13

Marion and I enjoyed our time at Westmoor grammar (although mine was cut short, due to another move of house). Our form teacher was a shy young man with floppy blonde hair, he couldn't have been long out of university, so was easy meat for the good natured teasing he had to endure.

His efforts to teach us German met with varying degrees of success and I am sorry to say I have forgotten most of it. What sticks in my mind was his obvious dread when launching into the lesson about the word "travel" or "Journey."

Unfortunately for the poor man , the word in German is "fahrt". The class fell about, whilst, beetroot faced, our teacher tried to instil some decorum into the proceedings.

The headmaster of Westmoor school at that time was a Mr. King, a tall thin man whom I remember only from the rather imposing figure he cut in morning assembly. The whole school lined up in silence in the hall whereupon Mr. King, complete with cap and gown, led his entire staff, similarly attired, down the centre of the hall and onto the stage. An impressive sight they were too in full academic regalia.

I am sure that seeing them thus instilled respect into all but the most hardened pupils.

The real power behind Mr. King's throne though, was his deputy head, Miss Elmer Mennie. I only found out her unusual Christian name years later, it never entered our heads at the time that she had such a thing as a first name, apart from "Miss".

She was a sturdy Scotswoman and definitely not to be trifled with She ruled the school with a rod of iron and the power of her formidable personality.

I enjoyed lessons there, apart from physics, which was completely bewildering and maths, which I had hated ever since my unfortunate introduction to it at Newburn.

Down The Town

At one stage, we got a new maths teacher at Westmoor, a keen young man who couldn't quite believe the extent of my inadequacy in the subject. He thought all he had to do was give me a little extra tuition and the veil of my ignorance would be lifted.

I have to say that he was very long suffering, but eventually had to concede defeat. He was quite crestfallen, poor soul.

<u>THE DAVISONS</u>

Marion and I took to visiting each other's houses at weekends, and so it was that I became an adopted member of her wonderful family.

The Davisons lived in a rambling old farmhouse and consisted of oldest sister, Edna, who, although not many years older than Marion and I, had a comfortable, kind personality, almost like another mother, and like her mother, had a head of hair the colour of a new penny. Next came brother, Malcolm, our elder by two years. Like Marion and their father, Rob, his hair was blonde and curly and his eyes were light blue, but whereas Marion's were tranquil, his held a mischievous twinkle.

The youngest member of the family was little sister Kathleen, only about five years old when I first got to know her, a brunette with pale green eyes, and a little monkey she was too!

Molly and Rob Davison

Marion's mam, Molly had the same air of serenity and common sense which Marion had inherited, but it was her dad, Rob, who was a revelation to me.

In our household, dad was someone we tip toed round. His every mood was watched as closely as a meteorologist watches the weather, indeed, his moods were as changeable as the local weather. I had become adept at reading the atmosphere and knew pretty well when it was safe to speak and when to keep quiet. Linda, on the other hand, either couldn't tell when it wasn't safe to speak up, or didn't care. Consequently, poor soul, she was permanently black and blue where my elbow dug her in the ribs to shut her up. I may as well have tried to stop the tide!

In the Davison household Rob was treated with affection without a trace of the wariness which hall marked my attitude to my own father.

It took me some time to get used to the idea that none of the Davison children were afraid of their dad and that this was the norm in most families. Indeed, I well remember the first time I stayed there. After the meal, Malcolm and his dad began to discuss the news of the day, each taking a different view point.

As their discussion grew more animated, I froze, waiting for the explosion of temper from Rob which would have been my father's reaction if any of the family had openly disagreed with him.

I was astonished when they rose from the table evidently still the best of friends. Eventually, I realised that father and son enjoyed a good argument, and if there wasn't one available, they would manufacture one and delight in the verbal cut and thrust which ensued.

Our German lessons turned out to be useful for Marion and I, as her mother, Molly decided to go on a coach trip to the Black Forest, taking both of us with her! What possessed Molly to haul two giggly fourteen year olds half way across Europe, I'll never know, but I am eternally grateful to her.

It was my first trip abroad, so it made a tremendous impression on me. I thought the Black Forest was the most beautiful place I'd ever seen. Because of its name I'd imagined a dark gloomy wood, when in fact it is similar to the scenic parts of Austria and Switzerland, but even more beautiful.

The bulk of the holiday was spent in a pretty little town on the banks of lake Titisee, where Marion and I, once we had stopped giggling at the name, had a whale of a time taking in the sights and flirting with the local boys.

We came unstuck once though. We had spotted two very attractive blonde haired, tanned, typically German lads and were discussing them in English, well within their hearing, not at all caring if they heard us, because we were sure they wouldn't understand. Imagine our horror when they began to talk to each other in English with broad Yorkshire accents, and walked away with a wave and a cheeky grin.

The fashion in skirts those days ran to extremes – you either wore pencil slim skirts, or more often for girls of our age, full skirts held out by many layered, tiered net underskirts. Marion and I used to stiffen our pink net petticoats with a solution of sugar and water. This did the trick all right, but had the disadvantage of making us the objects of fascination to swarms of bees. A decided minus when trying to present an image of cool sophistication.

Down The Town

My net petticoat let me down on that holiday too, on our way to the Black Forest we had a day in Brussels. All I remember about it is the statue of the 'Mannequin Pis', and a bit of a disaster in a very select store in the city centre.

Marion and I were sashaying around on our newly acquired high heels, well highish anyway, and full skirts with nipped in waists, feeling very chic , when I became aware of something catching on my heels. To my dismay I saw that the bottom tiers of my petticoat had come adrift and were trailing like pink net streamers behind me. There was nothing for it, I had to hide behind a fitment, step out of my petticoat and cram it into my bag, from which it kept erupting, like demented candy floss.

On the way back from that memorable holiday we stopped off in the city state of Luxemburg where Marion and I were naturally desperate to visit the famous radio station of that name. Bearing in mind that at this time there were no 'pirate' or local radio stations, all we had were the BBC Light Programme or the Home Service and about as funky as they got was the 'Billy Cotton Band Show' or 'Music While You Work'. So any teenager worth their salt tuned into the crackling, intermittent tones of Radio Luxemburg. Early on in the evening you had to sit with your head stuck to the side of the wireless to hear it, but as the night wore on it came in loud and clear and it was where all the latest pop music could be heard. Jimmy Saville, Pete Murray and Don Moss were all radio DJ's.

As luck would have it when Molly, Marion and I hove into view at the radio station, we were ushered into a small studio at the top of the building, just off one of the city squares, and warmly welcomed by the friendly fair haired figure of Don Moss.

It was quite strange chatting to such a familiar voice, and actually seeing it with a face attached. Between introducing the records he asked us about where we came from, our taste in music etc. and dedicated a record to us there and then.

"If you hang on a minute, I'm nearly finished here and I'll take you for a coffee." He said. To our amazement, ten minutes later there we were, seated at one of the many umbrella shaded tables in the middle of a quaint tree lined Luxemburg square chatting to one of the most famous radio presenters of the day. It was the first time I'd tasted real coffee and to be honest, I wasn't that impressed, but Don Moss treated Marion and I as though we were on a par with Molly and all of us as though we were visiting VIP's so we felt quite the young ladies.

With hindsight, it was kind of both adults, Molly had very little idea who Don Moss was and had never heard Radio Luxemburg, yet she took us there. Don Moss did not know us from Adam, yet he took time out of his evening to give to two 14 year olds and the mother of one of them.

DOWN THE TOWN

Although school and homework took up most of my time, there was the occasional trip down the town to enjoy.

Sometimes Marion and I would meet on a Saturday evening and hang about outside the stage doors of whichever venue the latest pop stars were playing, hoping to pounce on them and collect their autographs. Lord alone knows what dangers we would encounter doing that sort of thing now, but it seemed perfectly safe then.

We couldn't afford tickets for the actual shows, but the air of bonhomie among autograph hunters was such that there was never a dull moment, with the added frisson that the object of our devotion could appear at any moment.

Sometimes the supporting acts were all we saw, but we collected their autographs anyway, on the grounds that they might be top stars some day. Des O Connor was one such encounter. He emerged from the stage door of the Newcastle Empire on his way for a swift half between performances, and amiably signed our books, looking exactly the same then as he does now, even to the orange tan!

Johnny Duncan, (he of the Blue grass boys,) was particularly kind. After signing our books , he vanished into the pub at the rear of the Empire, to return within minutes with glasses of orange juice for the small group of young fans at the stage door.

One of the Everly brothers owes his continued existence to the fact that Marion and I were outside the stage door of the City Hall when they appeared there. They were at the peak of their popularity, so the group of autograph hunters had been considerably swollen by a large crowd of fans. This crowd rapidly took on the aspect of a mob when a coach drew up and a large group of musicians got off and entered the stage door.

The two brothers emerged last, accompanied by a manager or roadie or some such person. I had time to glimpse two slight figures with pale anxious faces and thick hair before the mob descended upon them with every appearance of being determined to claim a piece each! The Everlys's companion got behind them, grasped them by the shoulders, and began to use them as a battering ram, propelling them towards the stage door. Phil and the "roadie" made it, but at the last moment, Don slipped and was almost on the ground, in great danger of vanishing beneath the feet of the mob and being trampled to death.

With supreme self sacrifice, I reached down, grasped him by the back of his neck, hauled him upright and shoved him through the door, which slammed in our faces with an air of finality.

I struggled with mixed feelings. On one hand I had "rescued" one of the biggest stars of the day. On the other, if I'd hung on to him, I wondered whether I could have tucked him under my arm and taken him home!

Marion and I were exhausted by our tussle with the crowd, and very cross with the man, presumably responsible for the welfare of the brothers, who callously used them as battering rams.

On another autograph hunting expedition outside the City Hall, Marion and I had my sister, Linda in tow. Connie Francis, the biggest female pop star of the day was our target, so when a large shiny black limo slid silently to a stop opposite the stage door, we approached it, autograph books at the ready and were enchanted by a fragile looking dark haired lady who signed our books with a smile here, and a friendly word there.

Just before heading for the stage door, she turned and gave the door of her car a push to close it. It would have closed too, if Linda's finger hadn't been in the way! Linda squealed with pain and Connie was immediately at her side with abject apologies and offers to take her straight to hospital.

On closer examination, and loud protestations from Linda, we decided that hospital was not necessary, but Linda had her hand held by Connie Francis while one of her entourage wrapped the bruised digit in a clean hanky. Marion and I were quite envious.

Occasionally, we actually managed to save up enough to see a show from inside the theatre. Our favourite seats were on the steps behind the stage of the City Hall. Because you got mainly a back view of the performers, these seats were cheap and therefore affordable for us. On the plus side, you were much closer to the object of your admiration than the people who had paid a fortune to sit in the front row. Bobby Darin was one singer whose rear view I became familiar with, but there were many more whom I have now forgotten.

One I do remember is Cliff Richard. Marion and I saw him at the City Hall, (from proper seats this time) when he was a supporting act for , I think, The Kalin Twins, those "When" one hit wonders of the day. Marion and I were smitten, so, when he returned to Newcastle some time later, a star in his own right, we had tickets for the show. Not only that, thanks to a friend, we were to be taken back stage to meet him! You can imagine the excitement! I remember the occasion quite clearly, in the corridor on the way to the dressing room we met Hank Marvin and Bruce Welch from the Shadows who greeted us with kindness and humour.

As we entered the dressing room, which was a large room, full of other members of the group and their entourage, Cliff stood up, walked across the room towards us and shook hands smiling and chatting pleasantly. I had time to notice that he had beautiful teeth and warm friendly eyes, then it was time to go.

We were on cloud nine all the way home, in fact, when we got off the bus at Prestwick road end to walk to the Davison's house, we screamed with excitement all the way to the back door!

Cliff and friends at Butlins before stardom beckoned

I also got a front view of Marty Wilde. There was a competition in the Newcastle Journal (or it may have been the Evening Chronicle) which I entered and won, some sort of Quiz, I think. Anyway, the prize was one ticket to the Marty Wilde show at the City Hall. I was worried that mam wouldn't let me go on my own, but it was for the early performance, so she did.

Children were generally allowed much more freedom in those days. Dad knew nothing about it, or I have no doubt he would have put the kibosh on it. In fact, as I grew older, life became more and more of a conspiracy between mam and I to enable me to have any freedom at all. Fortunately, dad didn't take too much interest in my goings on, so it wasn't too difficult.

Most of my extra curricula activities actually consisted of visits to the cinemas at Newburn and Throckley and occasional stays with the Davisons at Prestwick village, but I enjoyed my forays down the town.

IF ONLY

Don Everly nearly was mine!
I had him right there in my grip.
Oh why did I let my chance go
And allow him to give me the slip?

I helped to get him through the door,
Rescued him from a terrible death.
Imagine if I could have kept him
The thought makes me quite out of breath!

Down The Town

It probably wouldn't have worked,
He'd pine for his brother I bet
Unless I could capture Phil too
And then I would have the full set!

WAKEFIELD

The Police force of Northumberland County finally came up trumps and allocated father a place on the detectives' course.

It was a six week course which took place in Wakefield, Yorkshire. Since our family still did not own a car, this meant that father would be away for the whole six weeks! Linda and I were ecstatic! Six weeks where we could relax and not worry about what mood father was in!

Even mam seemed cheerful at the prospect. The great day came at last and we tried not to let father see our delight at his departure.

All week we spent happy evenings choosing what we wanted to listen to on the wireless or chattering happily without having to listen for father's approaching footsteps.

The house was a markedly more relaxed place, almost as though a long held breath had finally been let out.

Little did we know at the time, but across on the other side of town, another family of two little girls was distraught because their dad, a Newcastle City policeman, (Newcastle and Northumberland had separate police forces then) was going on the same course.

Their dad had a car, so he would be coming home every weekend, but his wife and children were still upset at his departure. Unfortunately for us, their dad befriended ours and gave him a lift home every weekend! The anticipated weekends of freedom from the spectre of father never transpired.

Father had a photograph of himself beside the offending car and its owner, whose name, I learned, was Ken Scott. I would cheerfully have throttled him if I'd got my hands on him then!

Father (holding racquet), Ken Scott (middle back row)

Unbelievably, years later, I became close friends with his two daughters, Maureen and Margaret, and Ken and his wife, Elsie eventually became our much loved next door neighbours. In fact the two families have been linked in many ways over the years, but it all began with that lift home that Ken gave father. I reminded him of the event frequently over the years, but eventually forgave him.

The detective training course at Wakefield was open to policemen from all over Britain and the British Commonwealth (we still had one then), so on one of his weekends home from Wakefield, father brought with him a policeman from Kenya, Mike Hawthorne.

Kenya was at that time in the throes of battling with the Mau Mau terrorists and Mike had some terrible stories about atrocities committed by them. Needless to say, these were not meant for our ears, but horrifying as the stories were, Linda and I were fascinated and furtively listened in whenever possible. Once we even found some photos left lying about.

They were of mutilated animals, hamstrung cattle mainly. The memory of those pictures stayed with me for a long time. The knowledge that the same things and worse, was happening to human beings disturbed my sleep for ages. Later, when some of the people responsible for those atrocities came to power in Kenya, I was appalled; however, this seems to be the way of the world.

I never heard what happened to Mike I expect he stayed on in Kenya, he was born there and had a deep love of the country and admiration for its people.

He used to tell us what fantastic athletes they were, running for many miles cross country at tremendous speeds and clearing five bar gates without breaking stride. I can hear him now saying,

"If somebody could just get those guys onto a track, they'd be unbeatable"

It turned out he was right!

BLAME KEN SCOTT!

Dad is going to Wakefield
Hip hip hip hooray
He's going on a training course,
Six weeks he'll be away!

What fun we'll have without him
We'll laugh and talk and play,
With never a worry or a thought
Of what he'd have to say

Well, that's what we thought anyway,
But SOMEONE with a car
Gave him a lift back each weekend
Right home here from afar.

I gazed upon the photograph
Of father and his lift
And wicked things I wished on him
I'm sure you get my drift!

Little did I realise then
That further down life's path
That Ken and I, good neighbours now
Would talk of this and laugh.

<u>ON THE MOVE AGAIN.</u>

Life at Newburn trundled on for a couple of years pretty much without incident, apart from the New Year's Eve party which took place at our house. Jack Armstrong brought his pipes and accordion, so the house was soon full of music, friends of my parents and drunken polisses. As soon as they came off duty, they homed in on the sounds of jollification issuing from our place. They were plied with drink by father and bowls of home made broth by mother, in fact, a good time was had by all.

One young probationer P.C. who made the mistake of calling in before reporting for duty, was discovered in the early hours, crawling about under our dining room table in full uniform, muttering,
"I've got a one o clock point."

This meant he had an appointed meeting place with a senior officer at one am. However, since he could remember neither the name of the officer he was to meet, nor the place he was to meet him, he ended up staying the night, snoring loudly on our settee.

Later that year, the news came like a bolt from the blue, we were to be moved again! This time, to the horror of Linda, mam and I, it was to the far end of the county, away from everyone and everything we knew.

We were going to the little market town of Wooler, at the foot of the Cheviot Hills. Not the Rothbury side of the hills, which we loved from happy visits to family in that area, (see "Up the Valley") but a place we knew not at all. However, we were used to accepting the will of the police force, whatever the disruption it caused to our family life, so we set about packing up our home.

The journey north seemed to last for ever and served to emphasise the isolation of our new position. No more quick trips down the town.

Our house in Wooler adjoined the police station, and meant a return to living on a slope, as it was situated half way down Church St., one of the steep streets which led up from the banks of the river Till to Wooler's high street. In fact the whole of Wooler was on a slant, being situated on an eastward facing hillside.

The police station itself was a large grey stone building with an external staircase leading from our back yard up to the courtroom above. The building incorporated the police office, the afore mentioned courtroom, two cells and our three bed roomed house.

Wooler Police Station and our house

The pile of rubble in the foreground was the remains of an old house which was cleared to make a car park.

Down The Town

On the opposite side of the street stood an imposing looking building called the Archbold hall. This had been built in times past as a religious meeting house by two sisters, the misses Archbold, but was now the local dance hall, (alas, since demolished).

Next to it was a small grassy hill surmounted by the sparse remnants of an old peel tower, a seat on which to rest and view the town below, and the war memorial. This little hill was known locally as the Tory.

Linda and I clambered up it and looked down on our new home.

A view of Wooler from 'The Tory'

Down The Town

Also Published by 'LORWIL Publishing'

Up The Valley
by
Lorna Laidler
ISBN 0-9546475-0-5

Set in Northumberland's Upper Coquetdale, in the late 1940's and early 1950's, a collection of stories and childhood memories of summers spent on the isolated farms in England's most northerly and sparsely populated county. A humorous look, in prose and verse, at a way of life which has now disappeared.
Illustrated with line drawings and old photographs.

Border Stick Dressers Association
'The first 50 Years'
by
Wilf Laidler
ISBN 0-9546475-1-3

This is a 68 page book compiled from the archives of the BSDA. The 12 centre pages contain coloured photographs of walking sticks and shepherd's crooks made by various members over the years, of all qualities, styles and materials.

Down The Town

Down The Town

Down The Town

Down The Town

Down The Town